THE

LAND OF GOLD.

REALITY VERSUS FICTION.

BY

HINTON R. HELPER.

BALTIMORE:
PUBLISHED FOR THE AUTHOR,
BY HENRY TAYLOR, SUN IRON BUILDING.
1855.

SHERWOOD & CO., PRINTERS,
BALTIMORE.

TO THE

HON. JOHN M. MOREHEAD,

OF NORTH CAROLINA,

These Pages are respectfully Dedicated,

BY HIS

SINCERE FRIEND AND ADMIRER,

THE AUTHOR.

PREFACE.

PREVIOUS to my departure for California, near and dear friends extracted from me a promise to communicate by letter, upon every convenient occasion, such intelligence as would give them a distinct idea of the truthfulness or falsehood of the many glowing descriptions and reputed vast wealth of California. In accordance with this promise, I collected, from the best and most reliable sources, all that I deemed worthy of record touching the past of the modern El Dorado, relying upon my own powers of observation to depicture its present condition and its future prospcots.

This correspondence was never intended for the public eye, for the simple reason that the matter therein is set forth in a very plain manner, with more regard to truth than elegance of diction. Indeed, how could it be otherwise? I have only described those things which came immediately under my own observation, and, beside this, I make no pretensions to extensive scholastic attainments, nor do I claim to be an adept in the art of book-making.

A weary and rather unprofitable sojourn of three years in various parts of California, afforded me ample time and opportunity to become *too* thoroughly conversant with its rottenness and its corruption, its squalor and its misery, its crime and its shame, its gold and its dross. Simply and truthfully I gave the history of my experience to friends at home, who, after my return, suggested that profit might be derived from giving these letters to the world in narrative form, and urged me so strenuously, that I at length acceded to their wishes, but not without much reluctance, being doubtful as to the reception of a book from one so incapable as myself of producing any thing more than a plain "unvarnished tale."

In order to present a more complete picture of California, I have added two chapters, that describing the route through Nicaragua, and the general *resume* at the close of my volume. All that I solicit for this, my first offering, is a liberal and candid examination; not of a part, but of the whole—not a cursory, but a considerate reading.

H. R. H.

SALISBURY, North Carolina, 1855.

CONTENTS.

CHAPTER I.

CALIFORNIA UNVEILED.

CHAPTER II.

THE BALANCE SHEET.

CHAPTER III.

SOCIETY IN CALIFORNIA.

CHAPTER IV.

SAN FRANCISCO.

CHAPTER V.

SAN FRANCISCO—CONTINUED.

CHAPTER VI.

SAN FRANCISCO—CONCLUDED.

CHAPTER VII.

THE CHINESE IN CALIFORNIA.

CHAPTER VIII.

CURSORY VIEWS.

CHAPTER IX.

SUNDAY IN CALIFORNIA.

CHAPTER X.

BEAR AND BULL FIGHT.

CHAPTER XI.

SACRAMENTO.

CHAPTER XII.

YUBA—THE MINER'S TENT.

CHAPTER XIII.

STOCKTON AND SONORA.

CHAPTER XIV.

VOYAGE TO CALIFORNIA VIA CAPE HORN.

CHAPTER XV.

VOYAGE FROM CALIFORNIA VIA NICARAGUA.

CHAPTER XVI.

MY LAST MINING ADVENTURE.

CHAPTER XVII.

THE VIGILANCE COMMITTEE.

CHAPTER XVIII.

BODEGA.

CHAPTER XIX.

THE DIGGER INDIANS AND NEGROES.

CHAPTER XX.

ARE YOU GOING TO CALIFORNIA?

THE LAND OF GOLD.

CHAPTER I.

CALIFORNIA UNVEILED.

An intelligent and patriotic curiosity will find the history of few countries more interesting than that of California—which has at length realized those dreams of El Dorado that beguiled so many an early adventurer from the comforts and bliss of his fireside, to delude and destroy him. The marshes of the Orinoco, the Keys of Florida, and the hills of Mexico cover the bones of many of these original speculators in the minerals of the Western World. They sought wealth, and found graves. How many of the modern devotees of Mammon have done better in our newly opened land of gold?

To explain the causes of the frequent disappointment of these cherished hopes; to determine the true value of this modern El Dorado; to exhibit the prominent features of California and its principal cities, particularly San Francisco, and thus to enable those who still encourage golden dreams to form a proper estimate of their chances of success, without submitting to the painful teachings of experience—these have been the motives which have actuated the author of the present work.

The less to weary the reader, the book has been broken up into chapters, in which the author proposes to discourse familiarly upon what he has seen and felt, as he would in a friendly letter, rather than to write a formal essay or treatise upon California. In pursuing this plan, it is his intention to confine himself exclusively to facts, and to describe those facts as clearly as possible, so as to leave no ground for a conjectural filling up of those outlines which his negligence may have left vague and indistinct.

In this country, where almost every event that occurs is as momentous and unaccountable as the wonderful exploits of Habib's and Aladdin's genii, to deal with any thing aside from actual matters of fact, is at once as silly and profitless a business as that of whistling against the winds. Yet, in nine-tenths of the descriptions of life and times in California, truth and facts have been set aside, and the writers, instead of confining themselves to a faithful delineation of that which actually exists, have made astonishing and unwarranted drafts upon their imaginations. Instead of detailing facts, they have written fictions; instead of making a true record, they have interwoven falsehoods with the very web of their story. They have chronicled dreams instead of realities, and have registered vagaries as actual events and undeniable certainties. But they have themselves been deceived. They have been duped in listening to the delusive whispers of mischievous sirens, whose flattering suggestions and plausible stories have had such a magical influence upon their excited minds, that they have become accustomed to consider every thought of wealth that occurs to them a veritable mountain of gold;—that is to say, they have, by some strange hallucination, been converted to the belief that whatever California ought to be for their own particular ends and interests, it really is. In the night-time they have arranged and matured prodigious plans of profit, and although many days have dawned upon them since, that time has yet to come which shall reveal to them the utter nothingness of their nocturnal reveries. But the day will come, and it is fast approaching, when the spell must be broken. The iron utensils, which have been transmuted into golden urns and palaces night after night, shall once and for ever resume their true quality at the approach of day. The spell-bound shall be freed! The reverie shall be dissipated, the false wealth analyzed, and resolved into its component parts; and when these things are done, California will be seen in its true light. Then the eyes of the people will be opened. The golden haze which has hung over this land of romantic hopes and deadly disappointments will then be rolled away, and the clear, naked sunlight of Truth will shine upon this ugly cheat, revealing it in all its naked deformity to the eyes of the abused and misinformed public. Then, and not till then, will the full extent of popular delusion on this topic be known, and this mighty genie collapse into its original caldron.

The truth is, California has been much overrated and much overdone. She has been pressed beyond her limits and capacities. Her managers have been rash, prodigal and incompetent, and they have embarrassed her beyond hope of relief—though, it must be acknowledged, her condition was never very hopeful, but, on the contrary, I may say with the poet, she was only "half made up." It is plain to be seen that she was never finished. She has never paid for herself. An overwhelming public debt now rests upon her shoulders, and she has nothing to show for it. She is bankrupt. Her resources are being rapidly exhausted, and there is but lank promise in the future. Her spacious harbors and geographical position are her true wealth; her gold fields and arid hills are her poverty. But commodious and safe as are her harbors when once entered, they are not the easiest nor safest of access in the world, as I shall hereafter prove by statistics of vessels wrecked upon this coast within the last six years. And, before I finish, I shall offer other statistical information of interest and importance relative to the State at large, in substantiation as well of what I have already said as of that which I have yet to say. I may remark here that, my curiosity having led me to collect and prepare these statistics with no little care and attention, and at no trifling sacrifice of time and means, they may be relied upon as correct.

A residence of nearly three years, during which time I have traveled over a wide extent of those parts of the State which are most highly esteemed for agriculture and minerals, has, I claim, enabled me to arrive at a pretty accurate estimate of her character and capacities; and I have no hesitation in avowing it as my candid opinion (and I have not been a very inattentive observer) that, balancing resource against defect, and comparing territory with territory, California is the poorest State in the Union. She has little to recommend her except her fascinating metal, the acquisition of which, however, in its first or natural state, seems always to require a greater sacrifice of moral and physical wealth than a single exchange of it afterwards can possibly restore. I know it has been published to the world that this country possesses extraordinary agricultural abilities; but this is an assertion wholly gratuitous, and not susceptible of demonstration. Taken altogether, it is no such thing. Some of her valleys are, indeed, exceedingly fertile; but, when we compare their superficies with the area of the State, we find they are but as oases in a desert. I seriously believe that a fair and thorough trial will show that she has more than three times as much sterile land, in proportion to her territory, than any of her sister States. On an average, a square rood of Carolina earth contains as much fertilizing nutriment as an acre of California soil. Comparatively speaking, she has neither season nor soil.

No rain falls between the first of April and the middle of November, in consequence of which the earth becomes so dry and hard that nothing will grow; and the small amount of grass, weeds, or other vegetation that may have shot up in the spring, is parched by the scorching sun until it is rendered as easy of ignition as prepared fuel. The valleys above mentioned are the only spots exempt from this curse. On the other hand, from the first of December to the last of March it rains, as a general thing, so copiously and incessantly, that all out-door avocations must be suspended; and as there is no mechanical or in-door labor, either of use or profit, to be performed, the people are subjected to the disagreeable and expensive task of idling away their time in hotels and restaurants, at the rate of from two to three dollars per day for board alone, other expenses being in the same ratio. More of the disadvantages of this unfortunate inconsistency of the seasons, and of the paucity of resources of employment here, will be noticed as we proceed. As for the valleys we have spoken of, they will afford a sufficient supply of breadstuffs to support sparse settlements, but the average or general surface of the country is incapable of sustaining a dense population.

If we inquire after the manufacturing and mechanical resources of the State, we will find that she has none whatever; in this respect she is as destitute as the aboriginal settlements of America. Nor can she establish, encourage or maintain these arts, for the reason that she would be under the necessity of importing, not only the machinery and raw materials, but also the fuel. She could not, therefore, compete with neighboring States, which have at least some of these indispensable requisites. Nor has she any advantages or facilities for either water or steam power. How, then, can she obtain a reputation for manufactures and mechanism, having neither the material to work, nor the force or means to work with? She has neither cotton nor flax, coal nor timber. She is rich in nothing, and poor in every thing. She has to import every thing she uses, but has nothing to export, except her gold, which, instead of being a blessing to her, is a curse. Even the ground she cultivates she has to inclose with imported fencing wire, not having timber suitable for railing or paling purposes. That which is esteemed her chief treasure, dependence and commodity, gold, seems to be the least subservient to her advancement and prosperity; for, comparatively speaking, she sends it all away, and retains none for home use or convenience; and thus it is that she has, in a measure, been a benefit to others, while she has blindly and foolishly impoverished herself. In this she has acted upon the principle of the cobbler, whose shoes are ever tattered, and of the blacksmith, whose horses always go unshod.

But this profuse exportation of gold is significant of another important fact, while at the same time it demonstrates what I have said above. It shows conclusively that there is no inducement to invest capital permanently in this country, either in the prosecution of business or in the establishment of homes or residences. Immigrants find neither beauty nor gain to hold them here; and I feel warranted in venturing the assertion that not more than ten per cent. of the population are satisfied to remain. Of the other ninety per cent., the bodies only subsist here—their hearts abide in better climes; and they are anxiously waiting and wishing for the time when they shall have an opportunity of releasing themselves from the golden fetters which detain them, and escaping from a country which, with all its wealth, is to them a dreary prison. Only a small minority of the few who are lucky enough, by fair means or foul, to accumulate fortune or competence, are induced to identify their lives and interests with the country.

But the women are almost unanimous in their determination not to make California any thing more than a temporary residence; and they have good reasons for this resolution. Besides the social depravity to which I shall presently allude, and which is sufficient to shock the sensibilities of any *man* of ordinary morality, there are hosts of minor annoyances, resulting from the climate and the geographical position of the country, that inflict peculiar pain upon female sensibilities. The mud, which is often knee-deep, keeps them imprisoned all the winter; while, in summer, the dust, as fine as flour and as abundant as earth itself, stifles the inhabitants, fills the houses, penetrates into every nook and corner, finds its way even into the inner drawers and chests, soils the wardrobe, spoils the furniture, and sullies every thing. Besides, California is especially infested with vermin. Fleas, ants, and all sorts of creeping things are as ubiquitous as those that tormented Pharaoh and his people, and quite as annoying. No house is free from them, no one can escape the perpetual martyrdom of their stings, or the annoyance of their presence. As the ladies are the special sufferers from these abominable little nuisances, their unanimous dislike of the country is not at all to be wondered at. In proof of this unanimity, I can only offer the fact that, in conversation with quite a number of women who have resided in this State, I have yet to meet with one who is willing to make it her permanent abode.

We have alluded to the winds, because they really are a peculiar feature in the meteorology of this State. In the summer time they blow with peculiar violence, and facilitate the spread of the great fires from which California has suffered so much.

CHAPTER II.

THE BALANCE-SHEET.

Let us now take a glance at the *pros* and *cons* of California in statistical form. I have said that the State is bankrupt, that she has never returned an equivalent for the labor and money invested in her, and that she has been represented to be a great deal more than she is in reality—all of which I now reiterate, and shall endeavor to demonstrate. To make out a perfect and complete account-current, or balance-sheet, exhibiting the State's entire gains and losses of time, labor, life, money, etc., would require such a profound knowledge of financial affairs, and of political economy, that it would puzzle Adam Smith himself; we will not, therefore, attempt accuracy or exactness, but, having sufficient data to sustain us in our position, we will proceed to make it known.

Without charging California with any of the enormous expenses of the Mexican war, or the check given to the increase of population which that war occasioned, we will simply make her debtor for the amount of purchase-money that was paid for her, and for the various sums it has cost to control, manage and maintain her since. And, to avoid that complication and multiplicity of entries that would inevitably result from an introduction of all the individuals, parties or countries that have had dealings with the State, and as a matter of convenience, we will assume that there shall be but two parties recognized in the transaction, one of debit and one of credit—California and the United States. This will be treating the subject as a matter of dollars and cents, and will enable us to see how much has been made or lost, as the case may be, out of this Eureka venture or speculation.

In the first place, then, California is debtor to the United States for her quota of the amount of purchase-money paid to Mexico for herself and for New Mexico, including contingent fund absorbed by Mexican claimants, as per agreement at the treaty of Guadaloupe Hidalgo, $10,000,000. In the next place, let us see how much she is indebted to the United States for labor. At the present time, her population is estimated at about two hundred and fifty thousand. It is but little greater now than it was in 1849. In '51 and '52 it was larger than it was or has been at any preceding or subsequent period. It would probably be fair to estimate the average population at two hundred and fifty thousand for the last six years; of this number, it is supposed that from thirty to thirty-five thousand are women and children, who have become residents of the State within the last three or four years. Admitting, then, that there are thirty-five thousand women and children, and deducting this number from two hundred and fifty thousand, we have a balance of two hundred and fifteen thousand men, whose service for six years, at say $225 per annum for each man, amounts to $290,230,000. The outfits and passage of these men—to say nothing of the women and children —cost, at the lowest calculation, $200 per head; so we find that the expense of transporting the actual laborers alone has been at least $43,000,000. We may afford to let this latter amount rest as it is; but when we take into consideration the fact that the steamers are continually crowded with persons returning from California, and that their places are filled by new emigrants, who have to purchase new passage-tickets and new outfits, it is quite obvious that the figures express much less than the real amount. Tho above sums added together constitute the United States' charge against California. We will add them together, and then compare the total sum with the amount of gold that has been produced in California.

Original cost of the country	$10,000,000
Labor	290,230,000
Outfits and transportation	43,000,000
Grand total	$343,130,000

Thus we see California is debtor to the United States three hundred and forty-three millions two hundred and thirty thousand dollars. Now let us examine the account which California brings as an offset to this amount. The entire yield of the mines up to the present time, January, 1855, has been about two hundred and forty-five millions of dollars. And this is all. We cannot credit her with any thing else that would not be equipoised or balanced by the capital, whether owned or borrowed, brought hither from various parts of the world, and invested in business and improvements, and about which nothing has been said in the bill of charges. Here, then, is the sum and substance of the whole matter:

The United States account against California...	$343,230,000
California's account against the United States..	245,000,000
Deficit....................................	$98,230,000

And now let us see how much money has been lost in and about California by casualties, accidents and mismanagement. The reader shall judge whether any part of the amount should be charged to the State. As for us, we shall simply feel it our duty to furnish the statistics. In regard to the expenses of Fremont's Battalion, of the Army of Occupation in '47 and '48, and of the wars since waged against the Indians—amounting in all to several millions of dollars, we will say nothing.

In the annexed table is an account of the various fires that have occurred throughout the State. It will be perceived that the date of occurrence and amount of property destroyed are both given.

FIRES IN CALIFORNIA.

Fire in San Francisco, December 24, 1849	$1,000,000
" " May 4, 1850	3,500,000
" " June 14, 1850	3,000,000
" " September 17, 1850	450,000
" " December 14, 1850	1,000,000
" " May 3, 1851	12,000,000
" " June 22, 1851	3,000,000
" " November 9, 1852	125,000
" " Sundry fires in 1853	265,000
Fire in Sacramento, November 2, 1852	10,000,000
" Sonora, June 18, 1852	2,500,000
" " October 14, 1853	300,000
" " November 2, 1853	50,000
" Stockton, May 6, 1851	3,000,000
" Marysville, August 30, 1851	500,000
" " September 10, 1851	80,000
" " November 7, 1852	150,000
" Shasta, February 8, 1853	225,000
" Nevada, March 10, 1851	200,000
" Weaverville, March 7, 1853	125,000
Sundry fires in different parts of the State, dates unobtainable	4,400,000
	$45,870,000

Freshets and inundations, in the Sacramento and San Joaquin valleys, have swept off or destroyed one million five hundred thousand dollars worth of property within the last six years.............. $1,500,000

The following sailing vessels and steamers have been wrecked upon the coast within the same period:

SAILING VESSELS—SOME WITH CARGOES.

Vessel	Amount
Ship Tonquin—December, 1849	$2,300,000
" Crownprincessen—February, 1850	
" Utica—July, 1850	
" Somerset—December, 1850	
" Oxford—July, 1852	
" Aberdeen—July, 1853	
" Carrier Pigeon—June, 1853	
" Eclipse—October, 1853	
" Jenny Lind—December, 1853	
" San Francisco—February, 1854	

STEAMERS.

Steamer	Amount
Commodore Preble—May 3, 1850	$ 50,000
Union—July 5, 1851	150,000
Chesapeake—October, 1851	50,000
Sea Gull—January 26, 1852	50,000
Gen. Warren—January 31, 1852	50,000
North America—February 27, 1852	150,000
Pioneer—August 17, 1852	250,000
City of Pittsburg—October 24, 1852	250,000
Independence—February 16, 1853	70,000
Tennessee—March 6, 1853	300,000
S. S. Lewis—April 9, 1853	150,000
Washington—1853	40,000
Commodore Stockton—1852	60,000
Winfield Scott—December 2, 1853	290,000
Sundry steamers and sailers, the names of which have been misplaced	850,000
	$2,760,000

The present public debt of the State—entailed upon the people by one of the most imbecile and dissolute legislatures that were ever assembled in an enlightened country—is three millions of dollars........$3,000,000

The debts of the three principal cities are as follows: The total amount of the indebtedness of San Francisco is $3,342,000. The debt of the city of Sacramento amounts to $1,500,000. The entire debt of the city of Marysville amounts to over $70,000	$4,912,000
Total	$60,342,000

RECAPITULATION.

Fires	$45,870,000
Freshets	1,500,000
Shipping	5,060,000
State debt	3,000,000
City debt	4,912,000
	$60,342,000

These figures show the amount of property that has been destroyed, or the amount of losses that have been sustained in California, by accidents, mishaps and mismanagement, within the last six years. I will, moreover, give a list of lives lost by violent measures during the same period:

Murders	4,200
Suicides	1,400
Insanity, (produced by disappointment and misfortune)	1,700
Wrecked and perished on the way per sailing vessels and steamers	2,200
Killed by Indians and died of starvation per overland route,	1,600
Perished in the mines and mountains of the State for want of medical attention and food, and by the hands of the Indians	5,300
Total	16,400

It may be urged that the State ought not to be held accountable for any number of these sixteen thousand four hundred unfortunates, who, for the lack of law and order in a majority of the cases, lost their lives by violent means. We leave the question entirely with the reader. It may also be urged that the State ought not to be charged with any part of the extraordinary losses by fire and shipwreck, notwithstanding foreign capitalists were the principal sufferers in both cases. This question we also submit to the decision of the reader.

But I deem it unnecessary to dwell on this part of my subject. In presenting the foregoing calculations, it has been my aim to show that California is a country of unparalleled casualties and catastrophes, and to direct attention to the immense losses which have been sustained in opening its mines of wealth. A large number of people, it seems, have got into the habit of estimating the gains without taking into consideration the cost or losses at all; and there are those, no doubt, who will attempt to find fault with the account which I have drawn up between California and the United States. Though that account is in the main correct, I admit that slight errors may here and there exist; for, as I remarked at the outset, the debits and credits are so numerous, and of such an intricate nature, that it would be impossible to arrive at the exact amounts without the greatest research and elaboration. If I have succeeded in undeceiving those who have heretofore regarded California as an unincumbered God-send, my object has been attained. I have endeavored to show that, though there has been a great deal of gold obtained in the country, it is not all clear gain, and that notwithstanding there are large deposits of pure metal, there are also huge masses of dross. Shallow enthusiasts have asserted that the United States would have become bankrupt two or three years ago, had it not been for the discovery of gold in California. A more preposterous opinion was never entertained. Equally as much wisdom might be found in the assertion that Great Britain would have been sold by the sheriff, if gold had not been discovered in Australia. As a further proof of the beggarly condition of the country, it may not be amiss to remark that, during the last session of Congress, the general government appropriated upwards of four millions of dollars for the relief and benefit of California; and her senators and representatives are still clamoring for additional favors.

For the benefit of the reader, and in confirmation of statements made in this chapter relative to the past and present of California, I give the following extract from the *Louisville Journal*, to which my attention has been called since the foregoing calculations and statistics were prepared.

COST OF CALIFORNIA GOLD.

"For the information of those persons who believe that the United States thus far have been benefited by the discovery of gold in California, we propose to submit a few remarks and calculations.

"After the close of the Mexican war and the cession by treaty to us of Upper California, the world was astonished by the announcement, toward the close of 1848 or the beginning of 1849, that immense deposits of gold had been discovered in that country. As soon as the truth of this report was established, vast numbers of persons, young and old, flocked to that country. There was a perfect stampede of people from every State in the Union. Property was sacrificed to raise money with which to reach this Eldorado, where fortunes for all were supposed to be awaiting the mere effort to gather them. The first injurious effect on the country was the sudden withdrawal of so much labor from the channels of production; it was mainly, too, that description most needed here—that is, agricultural labor.

"We are not in possession of the statistics requisite to determine with exactness the number of persons who have been taken from the old States and have gone to California. The population of that State now exceeds two hundred thousand. But as there is a constant stream of people always *in transitu*, either going to or leaving that country, the number of people withdrawn from the business of productive labor largely exceeds the population of that State. It is not our purpose to over-estimate the amount of labor that has been withdrawn from the old States, but we feel satisfied that it will be under rather than over the mark to say that from 1849 to 1854, each year inclusive, there has been an average of 150,000 persons who have been during that time either in California or on their way going or returning. The time is six years for 150,000 persons, or one year for 900,000 persons.

"Now, if we estimate the average value of this labor at $25 per month each, or $300 per year, we have ($270,000,000) two hundred and seventy millions of dollars as the value of the labor taken from the eastern side of the Rocky Mountains and placed on its western side. In addition to this, it cost on an average $200 per head as the expenses of the removal from one country to the other. This makes ($180,000,000) one hundred and eighty millions of dollars as the cost of removal. The sums together make the sum total of ($450,000,000) four hundred and fifty millions of dollars drained from the eastern side of the United States. To ascertain the amount of the gold obtained from that country, we propose to take the gold coinage of the mint. This coinage was in—

1849	$9,007,761	1852	$56,846,187
1850	31,981,738	1853	46,998,945
1851	62,614,492	1854, estimated	42,000,000
Total coinage			$249,349,123

"As these figures make the sum total of *all* the gold coined at the mint, and a portion of it is known to have been obtained from other sources than California, the credit will rather be in excess than too small; but still we propose to add to this amount twenty millions more as an allowance for unminted gold sold to workers in jewelry and plate and which has been consumed in the arts. The statement will then stand thus:

California, Dr.

To labor and outfits	$450,000,000
Credit by product of gold coin and nature	269,349,223
Dr. balance	$180,650,877

"*This shows that there is a balance due us in lost labor and capital of over one hundred and eighty millions of dollars.*

"So far as California is concerned, it is probable that this deficiency is replaced there by the value of property, real and personal, which the labor taken from this region of country has produced there.

"The injurious effect of this vast emigration has been felt in the undue stimulus it has given to the prices of produce, induced by diminished production and increased demand.

"Another bad effect of this gold crop has been the influence it has exerted in stimulating excessive importations of foreign goods. In the last six years the imports will exceed the exports three hundred and three millions of dollars. Commencing in 1849 with an import trade of only seven millions of nominal balance against this country, it rapidly increased, until, in each of the past two years, it has exceeded sixty millions of dollars."

CHAPTER III.

SOCIETY IN CALIFORNIA.

HAVING looked into the financial condition of California, let us now briefly consider the moral and religious state of its society. We know that we are undertaking an ungrateful and painful task—that we shall awaken the animosity of those who have an interest in enticing settlers to this golden region—that we shall provoke contradiction, and probably excite controversy; but we beseech Heaven to pardon us for speaking the truth, and challenge our antagonists to disprove our statements.

We cannot, indeed, pretend to disclose all the terrible iniquity of that society in the compass of a single chapter—the theme is too extensive, the facts too revolting. It requires space to unfold the scroll which records such damning facts—it needs time for the mind to become sufficiently reconciled to the hideous details, to be able to listen to them without impatience or disgust. We can, at present, do no more than open the way for a fuller exposition of the subject in subsequent chapters. Suffice it to say that we know of no country in which there is so much corruption, villainy, outlawry, intemperance, licentiousness, and every variety of crime, folly and meanness. Words fail us to express the shameful depravity and unexampled turpitude of California society.

How much of this is attributable to the metal which attracts the population, we leave others to determine. One thing, however, is certain; mining districts do not generally enjoy a very enviable reputation in any part of the world. Gold, especially, is thought to be so easily accessible, and the return of the miner's labor is so immediately visible, that it has ever attracted the most unthrifty and dissolute. Men who could not be induced to work at any thing else, will spend days and weeks delving for the precious bane, hoping against hope, and laboring with an eager energy which nothing else can excite, and almost any thing else would more surely reward. Hence, the immediate neighborhood of a gold-mine is too liable to be a sink for all the idleness and depravity of the surrounding country. How these evils are multiplied by the absence of individual proprietorship in the land, and by the remoteness of a mining district from the beneficial restraints of public opinion, any one who gives a moment's consideration to the subject will perceive.

The exclusive devotion of labor to this one pursuit is another cause of increased laxity of morals. In the Atlantic States, gold-mining is only a branch of industry, and not a very important one, compared with the other pursuits of the population; but in California it is the chief and almost the only occupation of the inhabitants of the mining districts; so that while, in the former place, the general virtue of the people keeps in check the particular vices of the miner, in the latter, the good intentions of the few are overruled and stifled by the vices of the many.

We must not, however, commit the mistake of supposing that all the depravity of California is attributable to the nature of its industrial pursuits. This is but one of the elements which assist in producing the deplorable state of affairs under consideration. There are others which spring from the character of the people, and the circumstances which have brought them together.

It must be borne in mind that all the adventurers to this country have come for the express purpose of making money, and that to this end every other consideration is sacrificed. They have come to "put money in their purses," and as a large majority of them are of a class who are rarely troubled by any qualms of conscience, they are determined to do it at all hazards. Mammon is their god, and they will worship him.

If it be deemed desirable to make further inquiries into this state of things, it is only necessary to philosophize a little upon the physical structure of society. A single glance at it will suffice to convince the most superficial observer that its ingredients cannot be compounded into a harmonious, perfect and complete whole. Will a panther from America, a bear from Europe, a tiger from Asia, and a lion from Africa, organize in peace and good feeling around the body of a fresh slain deer? If not, will the Americans, English, French, Germans, Chinese, Indians, Negroes, and half-breeds, greet each other cordially over a gold mine? These are problems which those who have leisure may solve as their reason dictates. In the present case, it is more my province to relate the condition of things, than to account for their existence; yet, in preparing statements upon a variety of intricate subjects, owing sometimes to the difficulty of making one's self understood, it is both consistent and proper that, now and then, a few remarks in the way of explanation should be given.

Another very important cause of this wild excitement, degeneracy, dissipation, and deplorable condition of affairs, may be found in the disproportion of the sexes—in the scarcity of women. At present, there is only about one woman to every ten or twelve men, and the result is what might be expected. The women are persecuted by the insulting attentions of the men, and too often fall victims to the arts of their seducers. Nowhere is the sanctity of the domestic hearth so ruthlessly violated as in California. For proof of this, we need look no further than the records of the courts of San Francisco, which show that, in the course of a single week, no less than ten divorces had been granted, while, during the same time, only two marriages had been solemnized!

Not long since, an English gentleman, of whom myself and others had purchased some real estate in this city, came to me, requesting that, inasmuch as his wife had left him the day before, we would not let her have any money on his account. After finishing his business instructions, he gave us the following history. Listen to it. Said he: "Four years ago, myself and wife, and six other men with their wives, came together in one vessel to this country. Shortly after our arrival, family feuds and jealousies became rife in the domestic circle of one of the parties. The man and his wife separated. Soon their example was followed by another couple, and another, and so on, until all the marriage ties of our company were broken, except those that happily existed between myself and wife. Left alone thus, and having been true to each other so long, and through so many opposing circumstances, I cherished the hope that we might remain together, and be true to the end. But, alas! my fond thoughts and anticipations have proved a sickly dream. My hopes have been blasted, my happiness wrecked, and my children disgraced and deserted. My wife, whom I loved and held dearer than all else on earth, the partner of my life, has been basely seduced. The last link that bound the remnant of our seven families together has been severed, and the consequence is, we are a disbanded and disreputable people. Cursed be the day and the incentive that started me to this damnable country!" These were his own words, almost verbatim; and he uttered them as if partly speaking to himself, and partly addressing me.

The total disregard of the marriage tie by the majority of the men of California puts the husband, who is foolish enough to take his wife with him to that country, in a painful and embarrassing position. Should the wife be pretty, she is the more liable to the persecution of attentions which will shock her if she be virtuous, and flatter her into sin if she is not. She is surrounded at once by hosts of men, who spare neither money, time, nor art to win her affections from her husband. What wonder if they often succeed?

Female virtue or chastity, in the conventional sense of the word, is known to every one, who is familiar with the internal history of society, to be a very complex idea. There are women who are chaste only for want of the opportunity to be otherwise. There are others who are kept chaste by the force of public opinion, the dread of exposure, and the general fear of consequences; while a third class preserve their persons untainted by an innate purity of soul, which shrinks instinctively from all indelicacy, and feels contaminated by an unclean thought, and degraded by a lustful look. It is not our business to inquire into the relative proportion of women embraced in these three classes. It is enough to know that they exist, to appreciate the effect which the society of California will exert upon them.

As for the first class, it is not necessary to speak of them. They fulfil their shameful destiny every where, and California only ripens their depravity a little earlier. It is the second class who suffer chiefly from the peculiar moral atmosphere of the land of gold. In the Atlantic States, hedged in by a healthy public opinion, guarded by jealous laws, flattered into chastity by the respectful attentions which that virtue ever commands, they might retain to their dying day that physical purity which satisfies the great majority of husbands. In California, however, these restraints are all removed. Public opinion arrays itself on the side of vice; the laws are powerless to punish the sins of impurity; and all the attentions the women receive are based upon the hope of their ultimate fall. How are such women to resist? Cut loose at once from all those restraints which kept them in the right way, will they not dart off into the devious paths of error and of sin? It is impossible that it should be otherwise; and the man who would keep faithful to himself a wife of this type in California, must have wealth enough to gratify her most extravagant whims, time to devote exclusively to watching her, eyes keener than those of Argus, and cunning sharper than that of Vidocq.

The third class—of whom, I regret to say, I have met with but few in the Eureka State—have also peculiar trials to undergo. Society in that country is a reproduction, on a large scale, of the morals of the courts of Charles II of England and Louis XV of France. Vice only is esteemed and lauded, virtue is treated as an idle dream, an insulting pretence of superiority, or a stupid folly beneath the notice of men of sense. People do not believe in it—they scorn it, they insult it; they consider it a mere avaricious attempt to dispose of venal charms above their market value, so that the chaste woman has not only to suffer the persecution of insulting proposals, but the doubt of that virtue which repels her pursuers, and the sneers and scandal of a depraved and debased community.

Many women, of conceded respectability in California, seem to have come out there for the exclusive purpose of selling their charms to the highest bidder. Others, of more honest hearts, have fallen victims to the peculiar seductions of the place, but I must be allowed to pay a tribute to the sex, even in this its degenerate condition. Paradoxical as the statement may sound, it is rigorously true that these very women have improved the morals of the community. Any one who, like myself, has had the opportunity of seeing California before and after the advent of these women, must have been struck with the decided improvement in society since their arrival. They have undoubtedly banished much barbarism, softened many hard hearts, and given a gentleness to the men which they did not possess before. What, then, might we not expect from an influx of the chaste wives and tender mothers that bless our other seaboard?

CHAPTER IV.

SAN FRANCISCO.

We will now pay our respects to the occidental metropolis of the United States, sometimes honored with the title of the Queen City of the Pacific.

It has not been more truthfully remarked that Paris is France, than that San Francisco is California. This is the grand mart in which all the travel, news, capital, business, and, in fact, every species of interest or employment that belongs to the State is concentrated—the nucleus around which every plan and project must first be developed before it can receive life, vigor, system and order. It is the fountain-head of all the tributaries of trade and traffic that flow through the State—the great trestle-board or chart of operations to which all the journeymen repair for designs and instructions to pursue their labors. It is the supreme tribunal and regulator of affairs—the heart, the life, and the stay of the State. Contrary to the general rule, in this case the city supports the country, instead of the country nurturing and sustaining the city; and this will continue to be the case so long as the country is under the necessity of importing whatever she requires for use. Until she becomes the producer of the bulk or major part of that which she consumes, San Francisco will retain this ascendency. Every important movement, whether of a public, private, political or commercial character, receives its impetus from this point; and owing to its advantageous geographical position, and the facilities and accommodation offered for shipping, I think it may be safely said that San Francisco will be a great city, although California can never become a great State.

In order to particularize a little, and to furnish the reader with a more systematic idea of the city, we will imagine ourselves in a vessel, some distance at sea, approaching the coast of California in about the lat. of 37° 45′ N. and lon. 122° 25′ W. This will bring us to the Golden Gate, the entrance to the harbor. This entrance is a narrow outlet, through which at least seven-eighths of the entire waters of the State find their way into the Pacific ocean. It can be so thoroughly fortified that no maritime expedition could ever force its way through it.

Passing through the Gate, we enter the bay, and find it to be one of the largest and finest in the world, dotted with several small islands, and abounding in excellent fish of every variety. Soon we arrive at Long Wharf; the steamer is run alongside, and we are in the Eldorado of modern times. Around us we behold an innumerable crowd of eager lookers-on, who have come down from the city to meet their wives, lovers, fathers, mothers, sisters, or brothers, as the case may be. The crowd is probably one of the most motley and heterogeneous that ever occupied space. It is composed of specimens of humanity from almost every clime and nation upon the habitable globe. Citizens from every State in the Union, North and South, Americans, French, English, Irish, Scotch, Germans, Dutch, Danes, Swedes, Spaniards, Portuguese, Italians, Russians, Poles, Greeks, Chinese, Japanese, Hindoos, Sandwich Islanders, New Zealanders, Indians, Africans, and hybrids—all stand before us. We see all grades and conditions, all ages and sexes, all colors and costumes, in short, a complete human menag erie.

By the sides of the wharves, and anchored in different parts of the commodious and noble bay, we see magnificent ships, barks and brigs from every nation of commercial note. But of all these majestic palaces of the deep, none are equal in beauty of design and finish, in grace, symmetry and elegance, or in excellence of quality, to our own American clippers. Thinking that it might be of interest to some of my readers, as a specimen of American marine or naval nomenclature, I have taken the pains to collect a majority of the names of these oaken chariots of old

Neptune that have from time to time entered the Golden Gate, freighted with merchandise from Atlantic ports. Some of the names are truly appropriate and poetic. Ten of them, as will be seen, have, as a prefix, the word "Golden." I have arranged them in the subjoined list in alphabetical order :

Antelope,
Archer,
Atalanta,
Aurora,
Bald Eagle,
Belle of Baltimore,
Celestial,
Challenge,
Champion,
Climax,
Comet,
Contest,
Courser,
Dancing Feather,
Dashing Wave,
Dauntless,
Defiance,
Don Quixotte,
Eclipse,
Empress of the Seas,
Eureka,
Fearless,
Flying Arrow,
Flying Childers,
Flying Cloud,
Flying Dragon,
Flying Dutchman,
Flying Eagle,
Flying Fish,
Game Cock,
Gazelle,
Gem of the Ocean,
Golden Age,
Golden City,
Golden Eagle,
Golden Fleece,
Golden Gate,
Golden Light,
Golden Racer,
Golden Rule,
Golden State,
Golden West,
Gray Eagle,
Gray Feather,
Gray Hound,
Herald of the Morning,
Highflyer,
Hornet,
Honqua,
Hurricane,
Ino,
Invincible,
John Gilpin,
King Fisher,

Mystery,
National Eagle,
Neptune's Car,
Northern Crown,
Ocean Pearl,
Ocean Spray,
Olive Branch,
Onward,
Oriental,
Orion,
Pampero,
Peerless,
Phantom,
Queen of Clippers,
Queen of the Pacific,
Queen of the Seas,
Rattler,
Raven,
Red Rover,
Reindeer,
Ring Leader,
Rip Van Winkle,
Rover's Bride,
Sea Serpent,
Seaman's Bride,
Shooting Star,
Simoon,
Light Foot,
Living Age,
Mandarin,
Matchless,
Messenger,
Meteor,
Monsoon,
Morning Light,
Mountain Wave,
Sirocco,
Skylark,
Snowsquall,
Southern Cross,
Spitfire,
Stag Hound,
Storm King,
Sun Beam,
Surprise,
Sword Fish,
Siren,
Tam O'Shanter,
Telegraph,
Tinqua,
Tornado,
Trade Wind,
Typhoon,
Viking,
Waterwitch,
Western Star,
Westward Ho!
West Wind,
Whirlwind,
White Squall,
White Swallow,
Wide Awake,
Wild Duck,
Wild Pigeon,
Wild Ranger,
Winged Racer,
Wings of the Morning,
Witch of the Wave,
Witchcraft,
Wizard,
Zoe.

Leaving the vicinity of the shipping, we wend our way towards the heart of the city. As we proceed, we observe many objects of interest that deserve more attention than we can bestow upon them at this time.

Degradation, profligacy and vice confront us at every step. Men are passing to and fro with haggard visages and heads declined, muttering to themselves, and looking as hungry and ferocious as the prowling beasts of an Asiatic jungle. Before us on either side, we see a group of boys, clad in slouched hats, dirty shirts, ragged pants, and shabby shoes, without socks, who have no regular business. Sometimes they sell newspapers in the morning, and in the middle of the day engage in various occupations, as, for instance, in peddling fruits, nuts and toys. At this time several of them seem to have met by chance, and they have stopped to discuss the times and the progress of events. If we were near enough, we should probably hear the right hand party criticising Madame Anna Thillon's last performance of the opera of La Somnambula, or of the Daughter of the Regiment; and those on the left giving their opinions upon the merits of Madame Anna Bishop's last oratorio or ballad concert. After disposing of all the actors and actresses in music, opera, pantomime, tragedy and comedy, or, perhaps, after bragging of the successes of certain amours or other youthful depravities, they rally together, and entering the nearest groggery, one calls for a brandy smash, another for a whiskey punch, a third for a gin cocktail, and so on, until all are served. Then, bowing to each other, they drink to the prosperity of Young America, to which school they all belong; and dashing their glasses upon the counter with as hideous and vociferous anathemas as ever passed the lips of an East India pirate, they separate, segar in mouth, and return to their respective avocations. Not unfrequently these vicious youths repeat their potations so often that they become thoroughly inebriated, and may be seen quarreling, fighting, and lying about the streets like hardened and inveterate topers.

The bales and stacks of hay and straw piled upon some of the wharves, deserve a passing glance, since they form the sleeping apartments of dozens of penniless vagabonds who are always wandering about the city in idleness and misery, and have no other place to rest, no bed to sleep upon, except these out-door packages of provender, into which they creep for shelter and slumber during the long hours of the night.

Continuing our perambulations in a westerly direction, we find ourselves at the foot of Commercial street, which runs almost due east and west through the centre of the city. This street we will pass up, paying attention as we proceed to some of the irregularities and peculiarities which distinguish San Francisco from other cities, and California from other countries. The first houses we see are from one to two stories in height, and are built of red wood, a very light combustible kind of timber that resembles the spruce or cedar. Oregon produces nearly all the building materials out of which these and most other houses and tenements in California are constructed; and I have been credibly informed that the red wood and fir trees in that territory grow from two hundred and fifty to three hundred feet high, and proportionally thick. In some of the remote and comparatively inaccessible parts of California these varieties of timber are also found, and are said to acquire the same gigantic bulk.

Most of the buildings in this part of the street are tenanted by those mysterious and avaricious characters whose arrival in this, as well as in other places, is always as inexplicable as that of the flies in summer, and whose exit is equally as unceremonious as that of the swallows in winter —no one knowing whence they came or whither they go—the Jews, those nomades of civilization. These erratic and money-loving descendants of the ancient biblical patriarchs seem to follow in the wake of all adventurous Christians and gentiles who wear those convenient articles of apparel denominated ready-made clothes. Preferring to travel the way after it is once opened, they are seldom known as the pioneers of a new country; and claiming to be conservative in their principles and opposed to aggression, they profess disinclination to encroach upon foreign territory; but after the battles are fought with the forest, the wild beasts, or the biped enemy, and peace and security established, they are ever ready to come in and partake of whatever advantages may have been attained. So it has been in California, so it is yet, and so it will always be here and every where else, with these homeless and migratory people.

They do not employ any of their time or means in advancing the permanent and substantial interests of the country. None of them engage in any sort of manual labor, except, perhaps, that which is of the most trivial and unmanly nature, such, for instance, as the manufacturing of jewelry and haberdashery. Mining, the cultivation of the soil, in a word, any occupation that requires exposure to the weather, is too fatiguing and intolerable for them. The law requiring man to get bread by the sweat of his brow, is an injunction with which they refuse to comply. It is a tax they are unwilling to pay—an enigma beyond their comprehension—they will not sweat. Dealing in ready-made clothing appears to be their peculiar forte; and this is about the only thing they follow in San Francisco—as I think it may be said to be their principal pursuit wherever they go, when they have not the means to set themselves up as pawn-brokers or note-shavers.

We observe that they have presumptuously usurped or occupied from four to six feet of the way on either side of the street, by building little wooden racks and projections in front of their stores, for the purpose of making a more conspicuous display of their marketable vestments in dry weather. In any other place than California such unjust appropriations of the streets of a city would not be tolerated; but here, where usurpation, illegality and confusion reign supreme, no attention is paid to it.

It has ever been the misfortune of the Jew to undergo the scorn and contumely of self-styled Christians, and indeed of all nations. Since the destruction of his ancient capital by the Romans, he has been an outcast in the world, the standing butt of the Gentile's scoffs. California is no exception to this general rule. But little respect is shown him there; and he is continually jeered by having applied to him such annoying epithets as Christ-killer, ham-hater and anti-pork-eater. But few of them have signs over their doors, as most men have who transact business upon their honor and reputation. Some of them buy and sell under assumed names; but in general their business is anonymously conducted. Bidding adieu to the cosmopolitan issue of Abraham, Isaac and Jacob, and leaving them in the peaceable possession and enjoyment of their "too or tree towsand monnies," we will take a glance at matters of more importance.

Higher up the street we come to a better class of buildings than the miserable little shops we have just left, and we get a fair view of the permanent and attractive architecture of San Francisco—the brick and stone structures. Many of these buildings are beautifully designed and symmetrically proportioned, and have fire-proof walls varying from sixteen to twenty-four inches in thickness. They are usually from two to four stories in height. One hotel is five stories high, being the tallest house in the State.

Probably no city in this country can boast of buildings so substantial and thoroughly fire-proof as those of San Francisco. Besides making the walls very thick, every care is taken to have the doors, window-shutters and roofs equally stout and incombustible; nor is this precaution at all surprising, when it is remembered that this city alone has lost more than twenty-five millions of dollars by fire.

Owing to the unusual dryness of the weather, the prevalence of winds in summer, and the inadequate supply of water possessed by the city, all combustible matter is rendered so inflammable that it is quite impossible to keep it from burning after fire is once communicated; hence the necessity of using brick and stone instead of wood. The amount of money invested in this durable kind of improvement, as will be seen by reference to the following statistics which I borrow from the Herald, is something over thirteen and a half millions of dollars—the number of buildings being six hundred and thirty-eight:

	No. of buildings.	Value.
Mason street	4	$ 35,000
Powell street	13	156,500
Stockton street	35	423,500
Dupont street	37	450,000
Kearny street	23	535,000
Montgomery street	55	3,500,000
Sansome street	46	1,036,000
Battery street	63	1,106,000
Front street	39	612,000
Davis street	3	85,000
Geary street	2	16,000
Sutter street	3	30,000
Bush street	5	144,000
Pine street	9	144,500
California street	47	1,230,750
Sacramento street	52	778,000
Commercial street	21	462,000
Clay street	28	593,000
Merchant street	15	348,500
Washington street	37	608,500
Jackson street	19	308,000
Pacific street	7	167,000
Broadway	10	145,000
Vallejo street	3	36,000
Green street	2	16,000
Union street	6	92,000
Greenwich street	3	35,000

Lombard street	2	12,000
Chestnut street	2	20,000
Francisco street	1	36,000
Market street	2	40,000
First street	5	76,000
Brannan street	10	50,000
Third street	4	44,500
Miscellaneous	55	307,000
Total	638	$13,618,750

It is a remarkable fact, however, that less than half of these improvements have been made with California gold. Ask the proprietors where they got the money which they have expended in the erection of these buildings, and they will tell you it came from the Atlantic States and from Europe. Those who occupy them, the merchants and business men from New York, London, Paris, Hamburg, Bremen, and other places, will testify to this fact. California gold is to the world much what Southern cotton is to the North; it is not retained at home to supply the wants of the people, to afford them employment, to enrich or embellish the country, but is passed into distant hands, and afterwards brought back at a premium. Thus the producers are continually drained, and the commonwealth necessarily impoverished by this unthrifty management.

These buildings are erected upon the most eligible and convenient sites, and form what is properly termed the business portion of the city —covering, probably, about one-sixth of its superficies. Almost all of the residences or private dwellings are built of wood, and are very frail and inelegant. It is the intention, however, of a large number of the citizens to take down the wood and substitute brick or stone, as soon as they get able, if that is ever to be the case.

To acquaint ourselves with the character of the speculators and business men in San Francisco would be a curious and interesting task. They are certainly the shrewdest rascals in the world, and a straight-forward, honest man, who acts upon principle and adheres to a legitimate system of dealing, can no more cope with them than he can fly. But notwithstanding their shrewdness, and I might say, in some instances, their excellent business qualifications, they exhibit less method and system in their transactions than any class of traders I ever saw. Whatever they do is done in a helter-skelter, topsy-turvy sort of way, as if they had just fallen out of their element, and were scrambling to get back again. They never take time to do a thing well, but are always going and coming, or bustling about in such a manner, that one would suppose they were making preparations for some calamitous emergency, rather than attending to the every day routine of an established occupation.

This restless disposition is characteristic of the inhabitants of every part of the State; the mind seems all the time to be intently engaged upon something in another place, and the body is always pushing forward to overtake it.

Pursuing this digression a little further, it may be remarked of San Francisco that, although she is indebted to California for her existence, she is no longer dependent upon the State for her support. San Francisco can now claim to be as much the city of the Pacific, or of the world, as of California. The commercial advantages she enjoys, her inviting harbor and central position, are far superior in importance to any benefit she is likely to receive from the interior. The profits she will gain from the whale-fishing fleet of the North Pacific, and from her trade with the islands of the South Pacific, with China, Oregon and Russian America, will place her in a more prominent and enviable position than it is possible for the State ever to attain.

Returning to our subject, we find ourselves as far advanced on our way as Montgomery street. The course of this street lies north and south through the middle of the most beautiful and wealthy part of the city; it is, therefore, both the Broadway and the Wall street of San Francisco. Every phase and trait of life and character is cognizable here. The dramatist who would study human nature here, would have an opportunity of striking out something new, instead of repeating the old creations of his predecessors, for surely never was there so varied a page spread out before the eyes of man.

While in this vicinity, we may observe men, who in the Atlantic States bore unblemished reputations for probity and honor, sinking into the lowest depths of shame and degradation. Others, whose moral characters are unobjectionable, have been pecuniarily unfortunate, and are driven to the necessity of engaging in the most menial and humiliating employments. Among the latter class, I might mention lawyers, who, to save themselves from the severe pangs of actual want, have been compelled to fish around the wharves for crabs, and to enlist themselves in the petty traffic of shrimps and tomcods. Ministers and physicians fare no better. In a certain hotel in this city, not long since, a lawyer was employed as a regular runner; in another, adjacent to it, a physician was engaged to pare potatoes and wash dishes; while in a neighboring restaurant, a preacher was hired to wait upon the customers and clean off the tables. Now, does not every reasonable man know that these professional men did not voluntarily follow these inferior pursuits? It was not a matter of choice with them. They could not help themselves; they were out of money, out of employment, destitute of friends, and were compelled to take advantage of the first opportunity that offered of earning their daily bread. Half the lowest and most servile situations or offices in this and other cities in the State are filled, often without any other remuneration, than board and lodging, by these unlucky and depressed adventurers.

New as the country is, the dandy, that exquisite flower of a finished civilization, is not unknown. He may be seen at any time sunning his external splendor on the side-walk, and scorning his more useful cotemporaries as loftily as though he were promenading Broadway or the Champs Elysees.

Together with bankers, stock-jobbers, and other moneyed men, we observe that the students or disciples of Blackstone, Coke and Story have selected this street for their offices. Considering the heterogeneous composition of society in this country, the loose and unsystematic transactions of every-day business, and the unsettled state of public affairs, it will be readily perceived that there is an incessant clashing of feeling and interest, and that the result is a great deal of strife and litigation. Disputes and difficulties relative to real property, and spurious or imaginary claims, keep the court dockets continually crowded; and the lawyers have rich and abundant opportunities for the exercise of their forensic abilities.

For the first two or three years after the settlement of California by the Americans, all attempts to organize or establish the civil law proved fruitless; and during this anarchical period no redress could be had, except by an appeal to lynch-law, in which case death was sure to be the fate of the criminal. Then the country had no practitioners of law, except those whose talents ranked far below mediocrity; but now the San Francisco bar can boast of some of the most profound and eminent jurists in the Union. It is probable that they have been more fortunate in accumulating wealth, than any other class of men. Much of their business has been of such a nature that they could mould it almost exclusively to their own interest, provided they felt inclined to take such an advantage of their clients; and every body knows it would be a very unlawful thing in a lawyer to neglect himself. They are the largest owners of real estate in the city, and there is no species of property that yields so great a profit as this, if properly managed.

Land titles are now as much contested as they ever were, there being in some instances as many as half a dozen claimants to a single lot. The squatters cause most of these troubles. Generally poor, and homeless, they settle upon any vacant or unoccupied piece of ground that suits them; and as there is a numerous body linked together for mutual support and protection, it is an extremely difficult matter for the half-sustained civil authorities to remove them If the law were sufficiently forcible—if there were any such thing in California as sovereign law, these intruders would be brought to justice, and instead of the broils and butchery now so common all over the country, peace, safety and good order would exist. But as it is, no dependence can be placed upon the administration of justice; and unless a man takes the law in his own hands, and defends his person and property *vi et armis*, he must tamely submit to whatever injury or indignity is offered him. Sometimes several squatters settle indiscriminately upon a single claim; and in these cases, feuds, animosities and contentions are sure to follow; but the difficulties are soon arranged by a recourse to weapons, it being generally conceded that he is the rightful owner or claimant, who happens to possess the largest bowie-knife and the truest aim with rifle or revolver.

The grog-shops or tippling-houses constitute the last but not the least prominent feature of Montgomery street that we will notice at the present time. The devil has certainly met with more than usual success in establishing so many of these, his recruiting officers, in this region; for we cannot visit any part of the state or city without finding them always at our elbow. San Francisco might allot one to every street corner in the city, or in other words, four to every intersection of the streets, and still her number would not be exhausted. It is astonishing what an amount of time, labor and money is misspent in this nefarious traffic. Out of the two hundred and fifty thousand inhabitants in California, from twelve to fifteen thousand are exclusively engaged in this diabolical, but lucrative business; and, what is worse than all, nearly one-fourth of the bars are attended by young females, of the most dissolute and abandoned character, who use every device to entice and mislead the youthful and unsuspecting. Women being somewhat of a novelty here, their saloons are always thronged with customers, many being induced to patronize them merely for the sake of looking at them. What a base prostitution of their destiny and mission! Woman has come here, not only to pander to man's vitiated appetites, but also to create and foster in him unholier desires, and, if possible, to lead him further astray than he would have gone without her.

Lest we should fall in love with one of these sirens, we will not go near them, but will enter one of the saloons kept by a biped of our own sex. Across the street is a large and fashionable one, called the Blue Wing,

> "Where politicians most do congregate,
> To let their tongues tang arguments of State."

Adding ourselves to the number of its inmates, we find the governor of the State seated by a table, surrounded by judges of the supreme and superior courts, sipping sherry cobblers, smoking segars, and reveling in all the delights of an anticipated debauch. Another group of less distinction in public affairs, but better known to the proprietor because of their more frequent and protracted visits, occupy a second table in the back part of the room, where they are playing cards and carousing over a general assortment of distilled, fermented and malt liquors. The proprietor himself is a red-nosed, jolly fellow, of burgomaster proportions, generally in a good humor, who treats his victim-patrons with the utmost courtesy and politeness. He is every man's man, and always has a smile and a smart saying prepared for the entertainment of the bystanders. His two clerks, for he is unable to wait upon all his customers himself, are equally urbane in their deportment, and may be found at their posts from six o'clock in the morning till twelve o'clock at night, ready to flavor and tincture mixed drinks, to prepare hot punches, and to deal out low anecdote to vulgar idlers. On the shelves and counters are dozens of labeled decanters and bottles, filled with the choicest liquors and artificial beverages that the world produces; other articles of similar use and value are also kept for sale, and stored away in their appropriate places. As a minute survey of the bill of fare may not be uninteresting, I herewith present it:—

BILL OF FARE OF A CALIFORNIA GROGGERY.

Bowie Knives and Pistols.

Scotch Ale,
English Porter,
American Brandy,
Irish Whiskey,
Holland Gin,
Jamaica Rum,
French Claret,
Spanish Sack,
German Hockamore,
Persian Sherbet,
Portuguese Port,
Brazilian Arrack,
Swiss Absynthe,
East India Acids,
Spirit Stews and Toddies,
Lager Beer,
New Cider,
Soda Waters,
Mineral Drinks,
Ginger Pop,
Usqnebaugh,
Sangaree,
Perkin,
Mead,
Metheglin,
Eggnog,
Capilliare,
Kirschwassen,
Cognac,
Rhenish Wine,
Sauterne,
Malaga,
Muscatel,
Burgundy,
Haut Bersæ,
Champagne,
Maraschino,
Tafia,
Negus,
Tog,
Shambro,
Fisca,
Virginia,
Knickerbocker,
Snifter,
Exchange,
Poker,
Agent,
Floater,
I O U,
Smasher,
Curacoa,
Ratafia,
Tokay,
Calcavalla,
Alcohol,
Cordials,
Syrups,
Stingo,
Hot Grog,
Mint Juleps,
Gin Sling,
Brick Tops
Sherry Cobblers,
Queen Charlottes,
Mountaineers,

Brandy Smashes,	Flip Flap,
Whiskey Punch,	One-eyed Joe,
Cherry Bounce,	Cooler,
Shamperone,	Cocktails,
Drizzles,	Tom and Jerry,
Our Own,	Moral Suasion,
Red Light,	Jewett's Fancy,
Hairs,	Ne Plus Ultra,
Horns,	Citronella Jam,
Whistler,	Silver Spout,
White Lion,	Veto,
Settler,	Deacon,
Peach and Honey,	Ching Ching,
Whiskey Skin,	Sergeant,
Old Sea Dog,	Stone Wall,
Peg and Whistle,	Rooster Tail,
Eye Opener,	Vox Populi,
Apple Dam,	Tug and Try,

Segars and Tobacco.

The annual consumption of beer, wines and liquors in this State exceeds five millions of gallons, a vast deal of which is retailed at extraordinarily remunerative rates. All of the first class establishments, I mean those that deal in good qualities, charge twenty-five cents for every drink or dram they sell; but an adulterated article, of which there is always an abundant supply in market, can be procured at about one half that price. In some of the most popular and respectable saloons, genuine articles are always kept on hand for the benefit and accommodation of those who are willing to pay for a delicious (?) draught. I may not be a competent judge, but this much

I will say, that I have seen purer liquors, better segars, finer tobacco, truer guns and pistols, larger dirks and bowie knives, and prettier courtezans here, than in any other place I have ever visited; and it is my unbiased opinion that California can and does furnish the best bad things that are obtainable in America.

CHAPTER V.

SAN FRANCISCO—CONTINUED.

We will now look into Clay street, which intersects Montgomery, and runs parallel with Commercial. Next to Montgomery, this is the most fashionable street in the city; the large establishments where retailers deal in ladies' and gentlemen's dress goods being situated upon it. The side-walks are narrow, and generally crowded to such an excess as to render it really difficult and tiresome to travel them. To the ladies, shopping on this street is especially annoying and tedious; for they are designedly balked or hindered in their course by a set of well-dressed vagabonds, who promenade the *trestoir* from morning to night for the sole purpose of staring in their faces.

The following little circumstance, which occurred here about a year ago, will show that, however culpable it may be in those who make a regular business of gazing intently in ladies' faces, the act is sometimes induced by a natural and inoffensive regard for the opposite sex. A very clever married lady, whose notions and ideas of things were somewhat akin to those of the Merry Wives of Windsor, espied a gentleman gazing very earnestly in her face, when she turned to him, notwithstanding they were both on the street, and asked, "Why do you stare at me so hard, sir? Have I done you any injury?" "Oh! no, madam," replied he; "I assure you you have not harmed me in the least. But pardon me; I have been in the mines for the last two years, and it has been so long since I saw a lady, that I must own my admiration of you has compelled me to be somewhat rude in my scrutiny of your charms." The lady was satisfied with the complimentary explanation, and since that time has been more resigned to her fate, and better contented to endure the steady stare of the public.

The gambling-houses cannot be overlooked in a true sketch of life in San Francisco. One of the largest and most frequented of these, called the Diana, stands a few doors above us. The building extends, through the entire block, from Clay to Commercial street, and has a front proportionate to its depth. The doors, which lead into it from either street, are kept wide open from nine in the morning till twelve at night, during which time the hall or saloon is generally filled to overflowing with lazy men, of little principle, whose chief employment consists in devising some sinister plans of procuring a livelihood without work. On one side is a bar, attended by a *lady*, assisted by three young white men and two negroes. This is largely patronized by the occupants of the saloon—one-fifth of them drinking because they have been lucky, and the other four-fifths drinking because they have been unlucky. Around the walls are suspended showy paintings and engravings, some of them of the size of life, representing nude women in every imaginable posture of obscenity and indecency.

Seated around numerous tables, covered with cloth or velvet, and finished expressly for gambling purposes, are some rare specimens of greedy speculators in the folly of their fellow-men. The proprietor of the house rents his tables to professional gamblers at a stipulated sum per month, with the condition that he is to receive a certain per centage on the net proceeds of their swindling operations. Usually, two gamblers form a copartnership, hire one table, and station themselves opposite each other, so that each can understand every manœuvre and secret sign of the other; and when a good opportunity for cheating or defrauding presents itself to one of them, the other is always prepared to divert the attention of the audience or of the interested party from his partner's motions. Every possible variety of gaming that can be accomplished by cards and dice is practiced here; and every false and dishonest trick is resorted to (often with more than anticipated success) to fleece ignorant men of their purses. Lying on the top of each table is a pile of gold and silver coin, denominated the bank, the size and amount of which, as a matter of course, depend altogether upon the wealth of the proprietors. I have said "the bank" is composed of gold and silver coin; it must be one or other, or both of these metals in some shape—whether in dust, ingots, bullion, or coin; for these constitute the sole recognized currency of the State, there being no paper money or bank-notes in circulation.

At one of the tables we observe two proprietors, as before described. One of them is a lank, cadaverous fellow, with a repulsive expression of low cunning, full of hypocrisy and deceit, taciturn in disposition, unengaging in manners, who was formerly a Baptist preacher in Connecticut. The other has a vinous, fat, and jolly countenance, is open-faced, enjoys a joke, is lively, laughs at his partner for being so melancholy, is affable and courteous to strangers, talks a great deal, as might be expected, since, before he came to California, he was considered one of the most promising young lawyers in Mississippi.

The proprietors of another table are two old gentlemen of "three score years and ten," whose white hairs and wrinkled brows would seem to belong to a more honorable station in life than that assigned them by destiny. A third table is used by a couple of Spaniards, whose scowling brows and treacherous eyes indicate that they are better qualified for the transaction of infamous and atrocious deeds, than for fair dealing or magnanimous behaviour. A Jew and Jewess have command of the fourth table; the fifth is under the direction and management of a French *gentleman* and *lady;* a young American girl and her paramour have charge of the sixth; while the seventh, eighth, ninth, tenth, and so on, are presided over by sundry sorts of wicked spirits, unworthy of being named. Octogenarians, youthful and middle-aged men, married and unmarried women, boys and girls, white and black, brown and copper-colored, the quarrelsome and the peaceable, all associate together; and, at times, as might be expected, fight, maim, and kill each other with the same indifference with which people generally pursue their daily occupations.

I neglected to mention before, that, in some conspicuous point of the principal houses of this character, there is generally erected a stage or platform, upon which a company of musicians perform at intervals of a quarter of an hour. This they are employed to do for the purpose of enticing unsuspecting strangers and passers-by.

Like those engaged in the liquor traffic, these gamblers are a public nuisance, a burden upon society. They do no sort of profitable manual or mental labor; yet the community grants them a license to abuse the public, and to debase themselves. Their occupation being a discreditable and dishonorable one, it robs them of that degree of happiness and respectability which naturally belongs to every industrious and upright man. Like a deadly contagion, they blast and destroy all with whom they come in contact.

Thousands of these swindlers live by their expertness in gambling and tricks of legerdemain. Dissipated, reckless, and restless, they rove from place to place, rarely acquiring decent habits or becoming permanent citizens. They are, nevertheless, great lovers and admirers of women; and most of them make it a special branch of their business to cultivate a due share of female acquaintance. But we will now bid adieu to the blacklegs, and return again to the street, merely stopping a minute or two, as we pass out, to listen to the enchanting strains of "Katy Darling," or "Lilly Dale," played by the brass band in attendance.

What is here called the plaza, or park, which occupies one square between Washington, Clay, Kearney and Brenham streets, now lies before us; but as it is nothing more nor less than a cow-pen, inclosed with unplaned plank, we will say but little about it. In the middle is planted a tall liberty-poll, near which is erected a rude rostrum for lynch-lawyers and noisy politicians. If there is a tree, or a bush, or a shrub, or a sprig of grass, or any thing else in or about it that is green, or that bears the slightest similitude to vegetation, nobody has ever yet seen it; and, as a pleasure-ground, it is used only by the four-footed denizens of the city. On the east side of this delectable public square is the California Exchange, before the steps of which are stationed from fifteen to twenty French peasants, who pursue no business save that of blacking boots. Most of them have acquired or adopted this ornamental occupation since they left La Belle France.

A few doors above the Exchange stands the City Hall, which was formerly the Jenny Lind Theatre—a very neat stone structure, but wholly unsuited for the purpose to which it is now applied. The parties who built it for a theatre soon ascertained that it was a bad speculation, and became considerably involved in debt; and, to save themselves, and make the best of a bad bargain, they bribed a majority of the aldermen to purchase it for a City Hall, at several thousand dollars above the original cost.

In this way a monstrous swindle was perpetrated upon the community, by fraudulently appropriating the public money to the use and benefit of private individuals. But the fraud could not be remedied; the city officers had been elected as the representatives of the citizens, whose rights and powers had been vested in them, and if they were so base as to prove recreant to their trust, the penalty had to be paid by their constituents. They consummated their corrupt bargain for the theatre, the properties were removed, and, after the expenditure of much time, labor, and money, in making alterations and additions, the building was converted into what now stands before us—the City Hall of San Francisco. The principals in this iniquitous transaction enriched themselves and their accomplices at the expense of the city treasury, suffering nothing except the denunciations and execrations of an abused and outraged public. This is a fair sample of the disposition that is made of the public funds throughout the State. Sheriffs, treasurers, and tax-collectors, in the majority of cases, are expected to decamp with all the money in their hands, or to embezzle a part of it; and it has passed into a proverb, that no *honest* man can be elected to a city, county, or state office in California.

Were we to remain an hour or two in this vicinity, we should probably see a police officer rolling "a perpetual hymn to the Deity" on a wheelbarrow—for that, we believe, is Poe's euphemism for a woman. Intoxication is quite common among the ladies of this particular section of San Francisco, and the wheelbarrow, or some other vehicle, must be employed to convey them to the station-house, on account of the total failure of their natural organs of locomotion.

On the north side of the Plaza are some of the

best French eating-houses in the State. One of them, the *Cafe du Commerce*, which, translated into English, means Commercial Coffee-house, is quite famous for its choice gastronomy. A better dinner can be procured here than in an American house, because the French are better cooks, cleaner in their culinary arrangements and preparations, more polite and attentive to their guests, and less accustomed to adulterating their provisions. Dinner, without wine, costs two dollars for each person; but with it, from three to five dollars, according to quality and quantity consumed. The stranger cannot promise himself any thing very sumptuous or delicious in the way of eatables, even in the first-class hotels. He can get good wines and liquors, prime cigars and tobacco, and other accessory articles of superior quality; but the fare at best is very indifferent.

All the more substantial articles of food, such as flour, meal, beef, pork, and butter, are imported from Europe or brought from the Atlantic States. As these provisions are sent around by Cape Horn, they must pass twice through the tropics before they arrive in San Francisco; consequently, most of them become more or less sour, musty, or rancid, which, as we all know, renders them not only repugnant to the palate, but also injurious to health. But, notwithstanding their transportation of from seventeen to twenty thousand miles upon the Atlantic and Pacific oceans, old or fresh, sound or unsound, they must be sold, served up, cooked, eaten. They cannot be wasted or thrown away, for that would be a losing business, and people did not come to California to lose money, but to make it; nor does it matter to them whether they make it by the sale of sweet flour or by the vending of putrid meats.

Sour flour is sold at reduced prices to the bakers, who mix it with a larger quantity—say twice as much—of that which is sweet; then it is manufactured into bread, delivered to the restaurants, and devoured by the populace. The flour put up by the Gallego and Haxall mills, of Richmond, Virginia, receives less damage in its transit through the torrid zone than any other—at least, this is the reputation it enjoys in California, those brands being more highly prized and more eagerly sought after by bakers and consumers. Next to the Richmond, the Fredericksburg and Georgetown flour is most in demand. How it is that the flour manufactured in the localities just named, or in the vicinity of those localities, retains its pure and primitive qualities better and longer than that produced at the North, which, with few exceptions, spoils on the way, I am unable to say—unless, perhaps, the latitude or climate imparts to it a healthier condition or a preservative principle.

Within the last one or two years, considerable quantities of the cerealia have been cultivated in the low lands and valleys of this State, and a few flouring mills have been erected, which are now in operation; but the proprietors mix their grists so much with rye and barley, that the flour is less marketable than it would be if it was ground out of genuine wheat. To give character to their spurious compound, they practice a double imposition, by packing it in empty Gallego and Haxall barrels, which are clandestinely purchased and kept in readiness for the purpose. Thus they steal the reputation of the Virginia brands; and, by placing their falsely-labeled, inferior flour in the hands of their rascally agents, they succeed in effecting large sales of it to those who are not particular in their examinations. Though the fraud is easily detected when the barrels are opened, there is no chance of obtaining redress; for, in most cases, these deceptions are carried out in such an indirect or complicated way, through factors and agents, that it is too difficult a matter to trace them to their source. If, however, the guilty parties are discovered, it amounts to nothing; because here, where the laws are so loosely and imperfectly administered, where all strong persons do as they please, and weak ones must do as they can, it costs more to adjust a wrong than it does to endure it.

This system of cheating and adulteration is carried out in all ramifications of business; and if a man is not continually upon the alert, he is sure to suffer the penalty of his negligence, by having a worse thing than he bargained for thrust upon him, and that, too, without redress.

To return from our digression: although the French are somewhat more philosophic and scientific in their preparation of viands, we perceive no material difference between their mode of living and our own. They eat more slowly, are more graceful in their deportment at table, and seem to enjoy their meals as a feast, rather than to devour them as a necessary repast. Wine is their principal drink, morning, noon and night; and dinner to them, without it, would be as insipid and unpalatable as breakfast to our American grand-mothers without coffee. After the main part of the meal is finished, it is customary with them to sip a small cup of strong coffee, as a sort of accompaniment to their dessert. This, however, they do not flavor with cream, as we do, but use Cognac, burnt with sugar, instead. It is an unusual thing for them to drink water at any time, except when mixed with wine. I have the pleasure of the acquaintance of a very worthy and estimable French gentleman, who assured me that he had taken but one drink of crude water in four years, "and then," he added, "it make me sick."

CHAPTER VI.

SAN FRANCISCO—CONCLUDED.

After a night's lodging in one of the human-stables of San Francisco, called here, for politeness' sake, hotels, we feel sufficiently refreshed to continue our reconnoissance of the city. It will probably be as well for us to retrace our steps to the south side of the Plaza, where we re-enter Clay street, and ascend the long, high hill that forms the western boundary of the city. Before proceeding far, we come to a pistol gallery, on the left, owned and conducted by one Dr. Natchez, a short, thick-set "son of thunder," who keeps on hand the best assortment of dueling apparatus that the world affords. The proprietor's real cognomen is, I think, Brown, Smith or Jones; but every body calls him Natchez, because he came from the town of that name in Mississippi. He knows all about guns, pistols, and ammunition; is an excellent shot—can hit a bull's eye or a man's eye every time he pulls a trigger; and never fails to vindicate his honor when it is assailed. In the opinion of the duelist, he is emphatically an honor-saving man; and in matters of personal difficulty and dispute, there is no one so capable of giving suitable advice, or so well prepared to supply the necessary instruments of polite slaughter, as Dr. Natchez.

Among the fiery spirits of this Western Metropolis, the slightest affront, even though it may be purely accidental, is considered a wound to dignity curable only by an application of Colt's revolver to the breast of the transgressor; and as Dr. Natchez enjoys the reputation of preparing the best remedies for wounded honor, all those afflicted with the disorder apply to him for relief. Laying before him their ailments and grievances, he will at once say *the cause must be removed;* the offending party is waited upon with a challenge, which is accepted; and the Doctor, with commendable impartiality, superintends the preparation of the weapons for both parties.

Passing on towards the summit of the hill before us, we soon arrive at an elevation from which we have a clear and uninterrupted view of the whole city, which contains, it is supposed, from forty-five to fifty thousand inhabitants—about one-fifth of the entire population of the State. The original water-boundary of the city, on the east, was in the form of a crescent; but, the bay being shallow in this particular part, its shape has been changed, by filling it in with sand from the adjacent hills. Owing to the steep declivities of the original site of the city, this encroachment was demanded and effected by those engaged in commercial pursuits, who wanted level ground. The land thus made, being the most eligibly situated and convenient to the wharves, is far more valuable than that of natural formation. At first, however, heavy losses were sustained, in consequence of the insecure foundations of most of the buildings, some of which gave way entirely, and had to be reconstructed. Now, however, they understand it better, and take special care to pile and plank the foundation thoroughly before the superstructure is erected.

The process of filling up these water-lots was very irregular; and, as the work advanced, several ponds of water, which afterwards became stagnant, were cut off by these means from the ocean. In other places, the tide receded from the shallow parts of the bay, and from the surface thus left bare, as well as from the ponds last mentioned, there arose large quantities of highly offensive and almost suffocating gas, which obliterated all the painted signs in the immediate vicinity. Strange to say, the effluvium exhaled from these foul ponds and marshy places did not produce disease. The wind blew it off or counteracted its insalubrious effects.

Viewing the city from our present elevated position, we look in vain for any verdure. Indeed, there is not a shade-tree in San Francisco. Nor, if we search the outskirts of the city, can we find either trees, coppice, vegetation, or any green thing whereon to feast the eyes. The earth all around us is as sterile and unproductive as a public highway. We feel a void, as though a friend were absent. Nature wears a repulsive and haggard expression. Oh! how few there are amongst us who duly appreciate trees, those noble earth-fingers that point to heaven and uplift the mind to God! According to my judgment, there is a greater combination of the beautiful and the useful in a forest oak or hickory, than in all the gay exotics which are so carefully reared by the florist. I entertain no doubt that a large, luxuriant elm would attract more attention in San Francisco than a menagerie or circus; and it is a wonder that some ingenious and speculative Yankee has not, ere this, manufactured one out of soft pine and dyed muslin for public exhibition. As an instance of the feeling that exists here on account of the lack of trees, I may cite the exclamation of a distinguished gentleman with whom I once had the honor to dine. Said he, (his wife at the time being in North Carolina,) "I long for the society of trees almost as much as I do for that of my wife; and if she and a big oak could now be placed side by side within my reach, I scarcely know which of the two I should embrace first!"

Many other natural and artificial deficiencies and peculiarities, for which San Francisco is famous, might, with propriety, be considered before we quit our high retreat; but we will now conclude our panoramic sketch, and descend into the more densely settled part of the city.

CHAPTER VII.

THE CHINESE IN CALIFORNIA.

THE national habits and traits of Chinese character, to which they cling with uncompromising tenacity in this country, are strikingly anomalous and distinct from those of all other nations. There is a marked identity about their features, person, manners and costume, so unmistakable that it betrays their nationality in a moment. So stereotyped are even the features and form of this singular people, that we cannot fail in their identity in the rudest cut that pretends to represent them. Particular fashions and modes of dress give them no concern whatever. One common rule seems to guide them in all their personal decorations. All their garments look as if they were made after the same pattern, out of the same material, and from the same piece of cloth. In short, the similarity in their garb, features, physical proportions and deportment is so great that one Chinaman looks almost exactly like another, but very unlike any body else.

Let us now place ourselves in front of one of these xanthous children of the flowery land, and survey him somewhat minutely. Every one is acquainted with his method of dressing his head, which is closely shaven, except a small spot on the crown, about the size of the palm of the hand. Into this slender lock of hair thus permitted to grow upon the apex of his cranium, he interweaves long strands of sable silk, which form a cue that nearly reaches the ground. His hat, which possesses a brim of enormous width, is manufactured out of ratan or bamboo splints, and has an indentation made in the top expressly for the accommodation of his cue. He very seldom, however, wears this appendage tucked up in his hat, but generally allows it to trail about his back and legs, as young girls sometimes do ribbons. This pig-tail he loves as he does his life; and he would as willingly have his right arm amputated as part with it. Notwithstanding he carries it behind him, it is his character—the badge of his respectability; and Boodh or Josh alone could prevail upon him to cut it off. His coat, which is fashioned very much like a pea-jacket, is made of crow-colored cotton cloth, of flimsy texture, and buttons loosely around him as low down as convenience will permit. His pantaloons, the legs of which are a trifle smaller than a medium-sized meal-bag, are composed of the same stuff as his coat, and terminate at about the middle of his shins. His shoes or sandals—minus socks, for he never wears any—are hewn out of solid wood, and taper towards the toe nearly to a sharp point. As he moves along before us in these uncouth habiliments—his feet inclosed in rude wooden shoes, his legs bare, his breeches loosely flapping against his knees, his skirtless, long-sleeved, big-bodied pea-jacket, hanging in large folds around his waist, his broad-brimmed chapeau rocking carelessly on his head, and his cue suspended and gently sweeping about his back—I can compare him to nothing so appropriately as to a tadpole walking upon stilts! Ludicrous and absurd as this comparison may appear to some, no one who has seen him will say that it is incorrectly applied. Such, then, is something of the outline of the Chinaman; and, with but few exceptions, may be considered as illustrative of the entire race as seen in California. The few exceptions are the mandarins, who robe themselves in long figured gowns, and some of the wealthier classes, who wear silk and satin goods, instead of cotton fabrics. But the description given above will suit at least nine out of every ten.

According to the most reliable estimates, there are at the present time about forty thousand Chinese in California; and every vessel that arrives from the Celestial Empire brings additional immigrants. From a fourth to a fifth of these reside in San Francisco; the balance are scattered about over various parts of the State—mostly in the mines. A few females—say one to every twelve or fifteen males—are among the number; among these good morals are unknown, they have no regard whatever for chastity or virtue. You would be puzzled to distinguish the women from the men, so inconsiderable are the differences in dress and figure. The only apparent difference is, that they are of smaller stature and have smoother features. They are not generally neat in their outward habit; but on certain occasions, particularly on holidays, the *elite* doff their every-day costume, equip themselves in clean attire, and braid their hair into a kind of crest, which, as it is worn upon the head, bears a strong resemblance to the tuft of feathers upon the noddle of a peacock. Those who are from the extreme northern parts of the Chinese empire, are the ugliest and most rugged featured human beings I ever saw.

What the majority of them do for a livelihood is more than I can tell, as they have but few visible occupations. The laundry business affords those who live in San Francisco, and other cities, the most steady and lucrative employment; and in passing their premises, the eye is often attracted to such "Celestial" signs as the following: "Kum Kee. Washer." "Ahi Fe. Launder." "Wong Cho. Washing and Ironing—$3 per Doz." Catching and drying fish is another business in which they engage, but do not carry it on extensively; others are engaged in mercantile pursuits; and here and there you will find one in a public house, filling the place of a cook or a waiter. But, though most of them are held as mere slaves by their wealthier countrymen, it goes desperately against the grain with them to take the situation of servants among white people, as they are constitutionally haughty and conceited, and believe themselves to be superior to us in all respects. So exalted an opinion have they of themselves that they think they are the most central, civilized and enlightened people on earth, and that they are the especial favorites of heaven—hence they are sometimes called "Celestials." They look upon us and all other white-skinned nations as "outside barbarians," and think we are unduly presumptuous if we do not pay them homage! Out of the cities, more of them are engaged in mining than in any other occupation; but, as I intimated before, the majority of them lead a very inactive and unproductive life. Much physical exertion, however, is not required to secure them a maintenance; for their aliment, if possible, costs them less than their dress, which is by no means expensive. Indeed, so sparing are they in their meals, that it is seldom they eat any thing but boiled rice; and even this, which they bring with them from China, is very inferior to that raised in the Carolinas. It is an amusing spectacle to see one of them feeding on this grain. Holding a bowl of the rice in such a manner that the nearer edge of it almost touches his chin, and grasping two chopsticks, about the shape and size of penholders, between his fingers and thumb, he feeds himself with a lively and dexterous motion of the hand, not very unlike a musician playing upon a jewsharp, and continues the feat without intermission until he has finished. He seems to cram the food down his throat with these chopsticks, rather than let it undergo the usual process of mastication. The ardor and haste with which he executes the performance, remind one of a provident farmer when he pitches new-made sheaves of provender into a hay-mow, just previous to a thunder-storm.

The Americans salute them all indiscriminately by the easy and euphonious appellation of "John," to which they reply as readily as if they were addressed by their true names; and they return the compliment by applying the same term to us, equally indiscriminately. A great number of them think "John" is the only name white people have; and if they have occasion to speak to an American or European woman, they call her "John," too! But their own vernacular cognomens, like their language and habits, sound certainly very odd to occidental ears. The following may be taken as fair specimens: Kak Chow, Chum Fi, Yah Wah, Si Ta, Hom Fong, Dack Mung, Gee Foo. They are deplorably addicted to wasting time in games of chance; and there are a dozen and a half gambling houses in San Francisco under their especial control and direction. But neither Americans nor Europeans participate in the sports or fortunes of their tables; they themselves are the exclusive gamblers in these eighteen dens of rascality. Their money is chiefly composed of brass and copper coins, stamped with the characters of their alphabet. Hardened rice and stamped slices of pasteboard are also current among them as mediums of exchange.

Is this Chinese immigration desirable? I think not; and, contrary to the expressed opinions of many of the public prints throughout the country, contend that it ought not to be encouraged. It is not desirable, because it is not useful; or, if useful at all, it is so only to themselves—not to us. No reciprocal or mutual benefits are conferred. In what capacity do they contribute to the advancement of American interests? Are they engaged in any thing that adds to the general wealth and importance of the country? Will they discard their clannish prepossessions, assimilate with us, buy of us, and respect us? Are they not so full of duplicity, prevarication and pagan prejudices, and so enervated and lazy, that it is impossible for them to make true or estimable citizens? I wish their advocates would answer me these questions; if they will do it satisfactorily, I will interrogate them no further. Under the existing laws of our government, they, as well as all other foreigners, are permitted to work the mines in California as long as they please, and as much as they please, without paying any thing for the privilege, except a small tax to the State. Even this has but recently been imposed, and half the time is either evaded or neglected. The general government, though it has sacrificed so much blood and treasure in acquiring California, is now so liberal that it refuses to enact a law imposing a tax upon foreign miners; and, as a matter of course, it receives no revenue whatever from this source. But the Chinese are more objectionable than other foreigners, because they refuse to have dealing or intercourse with us; consequently, there is no chance of making any thing of them, either in the way of trade or labor. They are ready to take all they can get from us, but are not willing to give any thing in return. They did not aid in the acquisition or settlement of California, and they do not intend to make it their future home. They will not become permanent citizens, nor identify their lives and interests with the country. They neither build nor buy, nor invest capital in any way that conduces to the advantage of any one but themselves. They have thousands of good-for-nothing gewgaws and worthless articles of *virtu* for sale, and our people are foolish enough to buy them; but their knowledge of the laws of reciprocity is so limited, that they never feel in any need of American commodities.

Though they hold themselves aloof from us, contemn and disdain us, they have guaranteed to them the same privileges that we enjoy; and are allowed to exhaust the mines that should be reserved for us and our posterity—that is, if they are worth reserving at all. Their places could and should be filled with worthier immigrants—Europeans, who would take the oath of allegiance to the country, work both for themselves and for the commonwealth, fraternize with us, and, finally, become a part of us. All things considered, I cannot perceive what more right or business these semi-barbarians have in California than flocks of blackbirds have in a wheatfield; for, as the birds carry off the wheat without leaving any thing of value behind, so do the Confucians gather the gold, and take it away with them to China, without compensation to us who opened the way to it.

Still they are received with a flattering welcome. They are taken by the hand with an obsequious grasp, as if their favor was earnestly desired; and the impression is at once made upon their minds, that not only their own presence, but also that of as many more of their kindred as can be persuaded to come, is coveted by us. Their mining implements and boots (the only articles of merchandise they purchase from us) are sold to them at even less rates than to our own countrymen, more from curiosity than from any other cause. For some unaccountable reason, they are treated with a degree of deference and civility which is really surprising. To humor their arrogance and presumption, I have frequently seen Americans, in crowded places, relinquish the side-walk to them, and betake themselves to the middle of a rough and muddy street. Moreover, they are petted as if they were really what they preposterously fancy themselves —the most elevated and exalted of the human race.

But I am inclined to look upon them as an inauspicious element of society—a seed of political dissensions. They have neither the strength of body nor the power of mind to cope with us in the common affairs of life; and as it seems to be a universal law that the stronger shall rule the weaker, it will be required of them, ere long, to do one of two things, namely—either to succumb, to serve us, or to quit the country. Which will they do? Our people will not always treat them with undue complaisance. Their real merits and demerits will be developed, and such stations as their natural endowments qualify them to fill will be assigned them. They must work for themselves, or we will make them work for us.

No inferior race of men can exist in these United States without becoming subordinate to the will of the Anglo-Americans, or foregoing many of the necessaries and comforts of life. They must either be our equals or our dependents. It is so with the negroes in the South; it is so with the Irish in the North; it was so with the Indians in New England; and it will be so with the Chinese in California. The Indians, it is true, would not submit to be enslaved; but they had to suffer exile, hunger and death as a consequence of their intractability. Certain it is, that the greater the diversity of colors and qualities of men, the greater will be the strife and conflict of feeling. One party will gain the ascendency, and dominate over the other. Our population was already too heterogeneous before the Chinese came; but now another adventitious ingredient has been added; and I should not wonder at all, if the copper of the Pacific yet becomes as great a subject of discord and dissension as the ebony of the Atlantic. However, the discussion and consideration of these matters more properly devolve upon our public functionaries, who, I presume, if loyal to their constituents and their country, will not lightly regard them.

CHAPTER VIII.

CURSORY VIEWS.

CALIFORNIA has features as distinct and peculiar as the Alps or the Andes. It cannot be mistaken for any other country; it is like no other region on the face of the earth. Being new, and in some respects untried, the most various conjectures, and the most opposite opinions have been expressed as to its future fortunes and ultimate destiny. A few who have been successful in their schemes and undertakings, and whose interests and existence are now blended with it, flatter themselves that it is destined to become a great and flourishing state; while, on the other hand, the great majority, who have been disappointed in all their expectations, and thwarted in every attempt, pronounce it an unmitigated cheat, and curse it bitterly as the cause of their ruin. My own opinions are, I imagine, by this time pretty well understood. I speak of the country as I have seen it, not as a mere passing traveler, but as an attentive observer. I emigrated to it as much in search of adventure as of profit; and, during the three years of my residence within its borders, have had ample opportunities to explore and scrutinize it as I desired. I am fully satisfied with my information upon this subject. I have seen all of it that is worth seeing, and a great deal besides. I crave no further knowledge of it than I now possess.

While there is any unoccupied land between the British boundaries of Maine and the Mexican limits of Texas, between the Florida Reefs and the Falls of St. Anthony, I would not advise any person to emigrate to California for the purpose of bettering his worldly condition. I have, indeed, no personal knowledge of the other divisions of land west of the Rocky Mountains; yet an acquaintance with gentlemen of character and veracity who have visited those sections, justifies the opinion that none of them abound in those elements of exuberant and permanent greatness so characteristic of the States east of the Rio Grande and the Mississippi. Oregon and Washington territories, Utah and New Mexico are tolerable countries, and, in some respects, superior to California; but owing to the general inferiority of their natural advantages, they can never become as powerful or important States as Louisiana or New York, Georgia or Illinois. The Pacific sidè of the continent is, as a general thing, far inferior to the Atlantic slope.

In my judgment, the present condition and future prospects of California, so far from offering inducements for additional immigration, actually portend much poverty and suffering. The very fact that thousands of men, some of whom have been in the country from three to four years, are working for nothing but their board, is of itself justifiable ground for this apprehension. More than a dozen stout, sober, able-bodied men, who asked nothing in compensation for their services but food, have applied to me for employment in a single day. I have elsewhere remarked that many of the most menial and humiliating situations about hotels, stores and private residences are filled by these ill-fated men, who, if they had the means, would be glad to shake off the dust of California from their feet, and return to the homes of their youth, where peace, plenty and happiness are attainable by all. Misery and despair go to bed with them at night, rise with them in the morning and accompany them throughout the day; they have been grossly deceived; "hope told them a flattering tale," and broke her lying promise; their hearts are sick with unrelenting and consuming sorrows. Strangers among strangers, they have no friend to soothe or assist them in the hour of misfortune; if they hunger, they must fast; if sickness overtake them, death is their remedy. Depressed in spirits, and driven to desperation by bitter and repeated calamities, they betake themselves to the bottle for solace, become insane from extreme anxiety or over-activity of the

mind, or else, with bullet, knife, or poison, put a summary end to their wretched lives. Such is the history of many a man who has perished in that land of gold.

They left their homes flushed with hope; those near and dear to them imprinted the last kiss upon their cheeks, and bade them adieu with heavy hearts and tearful eyes, but found consolation in the hope that they would soon return. Those who escaped the many dangers of the various routes and reached their destination, wrote back to their friends immediately upon their arrival that all was well. The news was received with ecstasy; heaven was thanked for their deliverance from the perils of the trip; the neighbors were informed of the health and safety of the adventurers; and for a few weeks all things promised well. In a month or so another letter was anxiously looked for, but did not make its appearance; then fears began to be entertained, and the unwelcome thought would occasionally flash through the mind that all was not well. Nor was it. Month after month slowly and gloomily passed away, without bringing any tidings of the poor deluded wanderers; and it has now been so long since they were heard from, that it is easier to reckon the time by years than by months. Still their fate is wrapt in mystery which is no more likely to be unraveled than is the fate of the President and her crew.

All that can be concluded is, that they lie some where within the confines of California, with no monument to reveal the place of their final slumber.

The immigration to California has been too much like the rush of an excited and impatient audience into a theatre, when it is known that a favorite actor is about to perform. There has been too much scrambling, too much crowding and pushing. Every body has heard that gold is scattered over her hills and mountains; thousands covet it, and are foolish enough to suppose that any body can get it. Without taking a calm and deliberate view of the subject—without balancing both sides, or counting the cost, they have suddenly abandoned their homes, and rushed in disorder to the land over which hovered their visions of wealth. They imagined that they had discovered the secret of fortune, and, in their enthusiasm, immediately set out to realize their dreams. They discovered, alas! too late, that their emigration was ill-timed and unprofitable, that they had exchanged a good situation for a bad one, and that immense sacrifices must be made before they could replace themselves in their former position.

No country can ever become truly great, unless it possesses abundant agricultural resources; and as California is deficient in this as well as in other respects, it is absurd to suppose that she will attract attention longer than her mines pay for working. The banks of the rivers, and the localities in the San Jose, Sacramento, and San Joaquin valleys, form exceptions to this general sterility. There the ground is low and moist, or easily irrigated, the soil is extremely fertile, and produces vegetables, which, for size and powers of multiplication, have probably never been equaled. These spots, however, are little more, in comparison with the area of the State, than are the roads of a county to the county itself; and they cannot, therefore, be depended upon to supply the wants and necessities of the whole country, should it ever be thickly settled throughout—an event which, for the very reason I have mentioned above, I do not believe will ever take place. These valleys and the banks of the rivers seem to have become the receptacle of nearly all the virtue of the surrounding surface of the country. As a few specimens of the vegetable monstrosities, the productions of these fertile spots, that have come under my notice, I may mention a beet that weighed forty-seven pounds; a cabbage, thirty-two pounds; a turnip, twenty-six pounds; an Irish potato, seven pounds; and a water-melon, sixty-four pounds. Onions, lettuce, radishes, and other horticultural productions, also grow to an enormous size. Irish potatoes, however, I believe, are the most prolific crop that can be planted. Indian corn is cultivated to but little if any advantage All of the arable parts of the State are now settled; and farmers who go thither hereafter will either have to return, or abandon altogether the idea of cultivating the soil; for it will be impossible for them to make a subsistence out of the sterile hills of the upland.

That millions of dollars worth of gold have been taken from the mines, and that there is a vast amount still remaining, no one pretends to deny; but then it does not exist in the quantity that is generally supposed. There is nothing more uncertain, as a business, than gold mining in California. It is, indeed, like a lottery—more blanks than prizes; and as every man has to take his chances, he must not feel too much disappointed if his luck leaves him with the majority. A few make themselves independently rich, and go home with flying colors; but where one does it, there are forty or fifty, at least, who, though equally sober, industrious and deserving, do not make more than their support, and very frequently not even that.

Half the stories afloat concerning "wealthy returned Californians" are exaggerated beyond the power of tongue to describe. A case or two in point:—A young man from the West, who had been mining between two and three years, and with whom I had become acquainted, started home on a certain occasion, with about one hundred and sixty dollars over and above his expenses. In speaking of his friends, I asked him what he was going to tell them when he got home. "Oh!" says he, "I shall not admit that I have made so little; for, if I do, they'll accuse me of having been indolent, of gambling, of drinking, or some other disreputable thing that I have never been guilty of; so I'll give out that I have made twelve or fifteen thousand dollars; and about the time I shall have got them all in a good humor, I'll take an excursion down to New Orleans, and thence to South America, where I am determined hereafter to seek my fortune." Thus, although he was honorable, and not addicted to habits of dissipation, he had not the nerve to tell the real truth of his own success. This shows how easily these exaggerated rumors are set agoing, and public ignorance imposed upon. The further people live from California, the more credulous are they of golden legends; and I am persuaded that the young man above alluded to had no difficulty in making his neighbors in the West believe he was worth whatever amount he chose to tell them he had made. Extravagant as this story may sound, it is not without a parallel. A man, who had accumulated from three to four thousand dollars, returned on a visit to his friends in the East; and, to test the credulity of the people, he put out the report that he had made five hundred thousand dollars. His story was received by the gaping neighbors without a doubt; and all at once our adventurer found himself the invited guest of nabobs who never knew him before he went to California, though they had seen him hundreds of times. I cannot close these remarks without offering a word of advice to the marriageable ladies. If you seek a rich husband, do not form a matrimonial alliance with an El Dorado Crœsus; for, in nine cases out of ten, a "wealthy Californian" is a poor man.

Admitting all that is claimed for California in regard to her mineral wealth, it affords no reason why every body should rush thither; nor is it any argument that it will ever become the land of promise which an enthusiastic imagination may picture. It is already a pandemonium; and it does not clearly appear how it can become an elysium.

The benefit of mines of the precious metals to the country in which they are found, is still an open question. The weight of authority is against them. The history of Mexico and Peru, in this hemisphere, as well as the new chapter which California is opening, cannot be quoted in their favor. It seems to be decreed that, the more oblique the route by which gold is reached, the greater is its value; while the more directly it is acquired, the more mischievous is it to the morals and the material wealth of a nation. If, as Joseph Bonaparte so happily remarked, "gold, in its last analysis, is the sweat of the poor and the blood of the brave," the more of these ingredients contribute to produce it, the richer is the result. The concurrent testimony of all ages proves that those nations who obtain their wealth by the indirect methods of agriculture, manufactures and commerce, are more happy and more prosperous than those who dig their treasures directly from the earth. This result is partly brought about by the great diversity of occupations which spring up in such a state of society, and give employment to all classes of the community; whereas, in a mining region, rich only in the precious metals, the resources of labor are fewer, and its tasks less diversified. The moral effect of sudden riches must also be taken into consideration. Few men can gaze undazzled at the splendor of a large fortune; and the more rapidly they acquire it, the more likely are they to grow dizzy in its contemplation. It seems to require time for a man to become habituated to the sight of wealth, in order to enable him to enjoy it with ease or dignity.

We cannot, therefore, conclude that the mere presence of gold is sufficient to advance California to a high position among her sister commonwealths. She produces the circulating medium of the country, it is true; and the intrinsic value of that medium causes the world to overlook the cost of its acquisition. We have endeavored, however, to set people right on that subject in the chapter entitled "The Balance-sheet," and shall not repeat what was there said.

We will not urge any complaint against the climate; for, in this respect, all classes and conditions of men can be suited, whether from the burning regions of Central Africa, or from the snow-capped mountains of Russian America. Along the southern line of the State it is oppressively hot, and, as a matter of course, is somewhat enervating; but in the north and northeast, among the mountains, it is extremely cold; and snow, to the depth of from two to ten feet, is found there as late as August. Large quantities of this snow are brought down to the cities, a distance of more than two hundred miles, by teamsters, and sold as a substitute for ice. The northern and southern sections of the State are, as yet, but little inhabited or known, except by the natives, who, like all other North American Indians, are ignorant of any thing beyond the limits of their own hunting-ground. In the middle or central parts of the State, the climate, as a general thing, is delightful, and, withal, highly invigorating and salubrious. Around San Francisco, particularly, during the winter season, when it does not rain, the weather is unusually mild and pleasant; and I have often heard it compared to the climate of Italy. It is not so agreeable in summer, because the dust and winds prevail to such a degree, throughout the dry season, as to become a source of extreme discomfort. The main objection I have to the California climate, as stated in a previous chapter, is the division of the seasons into six months of dry weather, which burns and scorches the earth so severely that nothing will vegetate; and six months of wet weather, during which time the rain falls so hard and so fast, that it is quite impossible to perform out-door labor. These two seasons are general—that is, they affect the entire State; but the temperature of the atmosphere varies very much, according to locality. In and about the latitude of San Francisco, it is rarely ever too cold or too hot; though the weather frequently changes, three or four times in a single day, from calm and warm to boisterous and cool, and from boisterous and cool to calm and warm again. In other places, where the days are intolerably close and sultry, it is necessary to have one or two blankets to sleep under at night. The remarkable aridity and unfruitfulness of the country at large, may be ascribed to the protracted drought of the summer, which begins in April, and lasts until about the middle of November.

CHAPTER IX.

SUNDAY IN CALIFORNIA.

The Sabbath in California is kept, when kept at all, as a day of hilarity and bacchanalian sports, rather than as a season of holy meditation or religious devotion. Horse-racing, cock-fighting, cony-hunting, card-playing, theatrical performances, and other elegant amusements are freely engaged in on this day. If I remember correctly, it was about two months after my arrival in the land of gold and misery, that I had the misfortune to become acquainted with a renegade down-east Congregationalist preacher, who invited me to accompany him, on the following Sunday, in a deer-chase. Throughout the country, and in the mines, shooting-matches and bear-hunting afford pleasant pastimes; gambling is also practiced to a considerable extent, though not so much as on other days. But we shall probably learn more of the manner in which Sunday is spent, if we confine our attention to one of the larger cities, San Francisco, for example. Here regattas, duels and prize-fights are favorite diversions; and the Lord's day seldom passes without witnessing one or the other, or both. Here, too, for a long time, gaming was licensed on Sundays, as it is yet on week days; but recently the city fathers have passed an ordinance prohibiting the desecration, and I believe their example has been followed by three or four of the other cities. There is no State law upon the subject.

Connected with a tippling-house, on the corner of Washington and Montgomery streets, there is one of the finest billiard-saloons in the United States. It is very large, and magnificently decorated, has twelve tables, and is furnished, I am informed, at a cost of twenty-five thousand dollars. To this place hundreds of infatuated men betake themselves every Sunday; and it is an unusual thing, at any time, to find one of the tables unoccupied. Every day of the week, from breakfast time in the morning till twelve o clock at night, this saloon, like many others of a like kind, is thronged; but the crowds are particularly large on Sunday, because people have more leisure on that day. Though, in this particular place, they are not allowed to gamble publicly on the Sabbath, they lose and win as much money in the way of secret wagers as they do openly on any other day.

What can we expect but an abuse of the Sabbath, when we take into account the contrariety of characters, tastes, dispositions and religions here huddled together? When we scrutinize society, we find that some of its members, the Chinese and other pagans for instance, know nothing at all of our system or division of time, and that they are, therefore, absolutely ignorant of the meaning of the word Sunday. There is no unity of thought, feeling or sentiment here; no oneness of purpose, policy or action. There is no common interest; every man is for himself, and himself alone. Society is composed of elements too varied and dissimilar;—it is a heterogeneous assemblage of rivals and competitors, who know no sympathy, and recognize no principle, save that of personal profit and individual emolument. Nearly all colors and qualities of mankind are congregated here. The great human family is, as it were, sampled and its specimens formed into one society, each communicating to the other his own peculiar habits, and each contending for the same object—the acquisition of gold. It is manifest, therefore, that there can be but little concert or harmony of action. Masquerade balls, cotillion parties and jig dances fill up the list of Sunday diversions. On Pacific street alone, the most notoriously profligate thoroughfare in the city, there are from twelve to fifteen dance-houses, in which the terpsichorean art is practiced every night during the week, but usually with greater zest and animation on Sunday nights. These fandangoes are principally under the superintendence or management of Mexican girls, of whom there is no small number in San Francisco and other cities of the State. Before I ever saw any of the Mexican ladies, I had heard the most glowing descriptions of their ravishing beauty; but I must either discredit the accounts, or else conclude that my ideas of female beauty are very imperfect, for I have never yet beheld one of them who, according to my standard of good looks, was really beautiful. Their pumpkin hues and slovenly deportment could never awaken any admiration in me, even in California.

Bonnets among them are quite unknown. Half the time they go bare-headed through the streets and to church, just as they do about their premises; but most of them have a long, narrow shawl, which is sometimes worn over the head, as well as the shoulders. This shawl is, in fact, an almost indispensable article of apparel, especially with the better classes, who never appear in a public place, whether in winter or summer, without it. They wrap it around their face, head and shoulders so ingeniously that spectators can not obtain a glimpse of any part of their features, save the forehead, eyes and nose; the mouth, chin and cheeks are cautiously concealed. There is a gross lack of consistency among these women. Notwithstanding they engage in the lowest debaucheries throughout the week, they are strict attendants of the Catholic church; and dozens of them may be seen any Sunday on their way to matins, mass or vespers, clad in habiliments of the greatest possible variety. If they can only get one fine, fashionable garment they think it makes amends for the bad material and ill shape of all the others. Nor are they particular to have their whole person clothed at the same time. I don't think I have ever seen one of them fully attired in my life; something was always wanting. Sometimes they may be seen promenading the streets, robed in the richest silks that were ever woven in Chinese looms, but when you gaze down at their lower extremities you discover them stockingless, their feet thrust into a pair of coarse slippers, which expose to view a pair of rusty heels that look as if no ablution had been performed upon them for at least three moons. The Mexicans, however, in most cases, are fond of aquatic exercises; and they have several bathing establishments in San Francisco, for the accommodation of the public, (at one dollar per head for each bath,) as well as for their own convenience and gratification. Unless I have been misinformed, it is a custom with the proprietors, when a gentleman retires to take his bath, to dispatch a female servant to his room to scour and scrub him off! As I resided near an American bath-house, I always patronized it in preference, and did not acquaint myself with Mexican usages in this respect.

Lately, however, women of pure and lofty characters have emigrated to California, and, since their arrival, there has been a gradual and steady improvement of morals among the people, and the Sabbath is now much better observed than it used to be. Soon after their arrival, schools and churches began to spring up, and social circles were formed; refinement dawned upon a debauched and reckless community, decorum took the place of obscenity; kind and gentle words were heard to fall from the lips of those who before had been accustomed to taint every phrase with an oath; and smiles displayed themselves upon countenances to which they had long been strangers. Woman accomplished all this, and we should be ungrateful reprobates indeed if we did not honor, esteem and love her for it. Had I received no other benefit from my trip to California than the knowledge I have gained, inadequate as it may be, of woman's many virtues and perfections, I should account myself well repaid; and I thank heaven that I was induced to embark in an enterprise which resulted in such a collateral remuneration. This I am constrained to say, because I fear I should never have had a full appreciation of her merits, had I not witnessed her happy influence in this benighted land. It was only after leaving a home where her constant presence, her soothing and animating society, appeared as a matter of course, and removing to a sphere where she had a better opportunity of displaying her power, that I could estimate her real worth.

"From woman's eyes this doctrine I derive:
They sparkle still the right Promethean fire;
They are the books, the arts, the academies,
That show, contain, and nourish all the world.

O, then,
For wisdom's sake, a word that all men love;
Or for love's sake, a word that loves all men;
Or for men's sake, the authors of these women;
Or for women's sake, by whom we men are men,
Let us love women, and ourselves be true,
Or else we harm ourselves, and wrong them too."

With the generous assistance and co-operation of the gentler sex, the various religious denominations have succeeded in establishing for themselves suitable places of worship in most of the cities and larger towns throughout the State. San Francisco now contains fourteen churches, two of which are Presbyterian, two Congregational, one Unitarian, three Methodist, two Baptist, two Episcopal, and two Roman Catholic. The Swedenborgians, Universalists, Mormons, and sundry minor sects occasionally hold service in public halls; and, if I recollect aright, the Jews have two synagogues. There is also a pagan temple, where the Chinese pay their adorations to Boodh, or to some other imaginary deity, whenever they experience a religious emotion.

CHAPTER X.

BEAR AND BULL FIGHT.

It was a beautiful Sabbath morning in November, when the bells aroused me from a dreamy sleep; but before arising from my couch, being lazy and inclined to muse, I allowed my fancy to recall my departure from Carolina with all its attendant circumstances. The hour alone would have suggested such meditations, for it was on a dewy morning that I bade farewell to the loved ones of my far-off home. I recalled the yellow lustre of the sun pouring his floods of golden light over the glistening tree-tops; the tender adieus, the streaming eyes, the murmured blessing. I remembered the sadness of my heart as I thought of the distance that would soon separate me from the friends and companions of my youth, and the high hopes which soothed my pain.

As I was thus pondering I heard the sound of drum, fife and clarionet; and stepping to the window to ascertain what was the meaning of this Sunday music echoing through the streets of San Francisco, I saw a tremendous grizzly bear, caged, and drawn by four spirited horses through the various streets. Tacked to each side of the cage were large posters, which read as follows :—

FUN BREWING—GREAT ATTRACTION!

HARD FIGHTING TO BE DONE!

TWO BULLS AND ONE BEAR!

The citizens of San Francisco and vicinity are respectfully informed that at *four o'clock this afternoon, Sunday, Nov. 14th,* at *Mission Dolores,* a *rich treat* will be prepared for them, and that they will have an opportunity of enjoying a fund of the *raciest sport* of the season. TWO LARGE BULLS AND A BEAR, all *in prime condition for fighting,* and under the management of *experienced Mexicans,* will contribute to the *amusement of the audience.*

Programme—In two Acts.

ACT I.

BULL AND BEAR—"HERCULES" AND "TROJAN,"

Will be conducted into the arena, and there *chained together,* where they will fight *until one kills the other.*

JOSE IGNACIO,
PICO GOMEZ, } Managers.

ACT II.

The great bull, "BEHEMOTH," will be *let loose in the arena,* where he will be *attacked by two of the most celebrated and expert picadors of Mexico,* and finally *dispatched after the true Spanish method.*

Admittance $3—Tickets for sale at the door.

JOAQUIN VATRETO,
JESUS ALVAREZ, } Managers.

Mission Dolores, the place where these cruel sports were held, is a small village about two miles south-west of San Francisco, which was first settled by a couple of Roman Catholic priests during the American Revolution. It is contended by some that this was the first settlement effected by white persons in Upper California. The buildings are but one story in height, covered with tiles, and are constructed of *adobe* or sun-dried clay. With regard to the general aspect of the place, it is distressingly shabby and gloomy. For scores of years, the inhabitants, who are a queer compound of Spanish and Indian blood, have lived here in poverty, ignorance and inactivity. But I am digressing. What was I to do about the bull-fight? I had never witnessed such an exhibition, and consequently had a great desire to see it. It was Sunday, however, and how could I reconcile the instructions of a pious mother with an inclination so much at variance with the divine command? Well, without entering into any thing like a defence of my determination, suffice it to say that I made up my mind to go, and went. Anxious, however, to moderate or diminish the sin as much as possible, I determined to hear a sermon first, and go to the bull-fight afterwards. For the sake of somewhat condensing the events of the day, I concluded to leave the city immediately, and repair to the Mission, there to attend an antique Catholic church, which has been built nearly three-quarters of a century.

Starting off with this view, I arrived within

hearing of the priests' voices about the time they began to chant the service, and on entering the rickety old church, much to my gratification, I learned that it was an extraordinary occasion with them, and that a deal of unusual display might be expected. The rite or ceremony of high mass was to be performed. Monks and friars from the monasteries of Mexico were in attendance; and the church was thronged with a large and heterogeneous crowd.

Four o'clock, the hour appointed for the fight between the bear and the bull, having arrived, a few taps by the drummer, and some popular airs played by the other musicians, announced that the amphitheatre, which fronted the church and stood but a few yards from it, was open for the reception of those who desired admission. I made my way to the ticket-office, and handed three dollars to the collector, who placed in my hand a voucher, which gained me access to an eligible seat within the inclosure. I found myself among the first who entered; and as it was some time before the whole audience assembled, I had ample opportunities to scan the characters who composed it, and to examine the arrangement and disposition of things around me.

The seats were very properly elevated so high above the arena that no danger was likely to result from the furious animals; and I suppose five thousand persons could have been conveniently accommodated, though only about three-fourths of that number were present. Among the auditory, I noticed many Spanish maids and matrons, who manifested as much enthusiasm and delight in anticipation of what was to follow as the most enthusiastic sportsman on the ground. Crying children, too, in the arms of self-satisfied and admiring mothers, were there, full of noise and mischief, and a nuisance, as they always are, in theatres and churches, to all sober-minded people. Of men, there were all sizes, colors and classes, such as California, and California alone, can bring together. There was but one, however, who attracted my particular attention on this occasion. I had no recollection of having ever seen him before that day. He sat a few feet from me on my left. There was nothing uncommon about his form or features. The expression of his countenance was neither intellectual nor amiable. His acquirements and attainments were doubtless limited, for he demeaned himself rudely, and exhibited but little dignity of manner. It was the strange metamorphosis he had undergone since the morning which won for him my special observation. Only four hours had elapsed since I saw him officiating at the altar and feasting upon a substance which he believed to be the actual flesh and blood of Jesus Christ, who died more than eighteen hundred years ago! In the forenoon of the Lord's day, he took upon himself the character of God's vicegerent, invested himself with sacerdotal robes, assumed a sanctified visage, and discharged the sacred duties of his office. In the afternoon of the same Sabbath, he doffed his holy orders, sanctioned merciless diversions, mingled on terms of equality with gamblers and desperados, and held himself in readiness to exclaim Bravo! at the finale of a bull-fight.

By this time the whooping, shouting and stamping of the spectators attested that they were eager and restless to behold the brutal combat; and an overture by a full brass band, which had been chartered for the occasion, gave them assurance that their wishes would soon be complied with. The music ceased; the trap-door of the bull's cage was raised, and "Hercules," huge, brawny and wild, leaped into the centre of the inclosed arena, shaking his head, switching his tail, and surveying the audience with a savage stare that would have intimidated the stoutest hearts, had he not been strongly barred below them. His eyes glistened with defiance, and he seemed to crave nothing so much as an enemy upon which he might wreak his vengeance. He contorted his body, lashed his back, snuffed, snorted, pawed, bellowed, and otherwise behaved so frantically, that I was fearful he could not contain himself until his antagonist was prepared. Just then, two picadors—Mexicans on horseback—entered the arena, with lassos in hand. Taurus welcomed them with an attitude of attack, and was about to rush upon one of their horses with the force of a battering-ram, when, with most commendable dexterity, the picador who was farthest off lassoed him by the horns, and foiled him in his mad design. As quick as thought, the horseman from whom the bull's attention had been diverted, threw his lasso around his horns also; and in this way they brought him to a stand midway between them. A third person, a footman, now ran in, and seizing his tail, twisted it until he fell flat on his side; when, by the help of an additional assistant, the end of a long log-chain was fastened to his right hind-leg. In this prostrated condition he was kept until the other end of the chain was secured to the left fore-leg of the bear, as we shall now describe.

Running a pair of large clasping-tongs under Bruin's trap-door, which was lifted just enough for the purpose, they grasped his foot, pulled it out, and held it firmly, while one of the party bound the opposite end of the chain fast to his leg with thongs. This done, they hoisted the trap-door sufficiently high to admit of his egress, when out stalked "Trojan," apparently too proud and disdainful to vouchsafe a glance upon surrounding objects. He was a stalwart, lusty-looking animal, the largest grizzly bear I had ever seen, weighing full fourteen hundred pounds.

It was said that he was an adept in conflicts of this nature, as he then enjoyed the honorable reputation of having delivered three bulls from the vicissitudes of this life. It is probable, however, that his previous victories had flushed and inspired him with an unwarrantable degree of confidence; for he seemed to regard the bull more as a thing to be despised than as an equal or dangerous rival. Though he gave vent to a few ferocious growls, it was evident that he felt more inclination to resist an attack than to make one. With the bull, the case was very different; he was of a pugnacious disposition, and had become feverish for a foe. Now he had one. An adversary of gigantic proportions and great prowess stood before him; and as soon as he spied him, he moved backward, the entire length of the chain, which jerked the bear's foot and made him rend the air with a most fearful howl, that served but the more to incense the bull. Shaking his head maliciously, casting it down, and throwing up his tail, he plunged at the bear with a force and fury that were irresistible. The collision was terrible, completely overthrowing his ponderous enemy and laying him flat on his back. Both were injured, but neither was conquered; both mutually recoiled to prepare again to strike for victory. With eyes gleaming with fire, and full of resolution, the bull strode proudly over his prostrate enemy, and placed himself in position to make a second attack. But now the bear was prepared to receive him; he had recovered his feet wild with rage, and he then appeared to beckon to the bull to meet him without delay. The bull needed no challenge; he was, if possible, more impetuous than the bear, and did not lose any more time than it required to measure the length of the chain. Again, with unabated fierceness, he darted at the bear, and, as before, struck him with an impetus that seemed to have been borrowed from Jove's own thunderbolt; as he came in contact with the bear, that amiable animal grappled him by the neck, and squeezed him so hard that he could scarcely save himself from suffocation. The bull now found himself in a decidedly uncomfortable situation; the bear had him as he wanted him. Powerful as he was, he could not break loose from Bruin. A vice could not have held him more firmly. The strong arms of the bear hugged him in a ruthless and desperate embrace. It was a stirring sight to see these infuriated and muscular antagonists struggling to take each other's life. It was enough to make a heathen generalissimo shudder to look at them. How ought it to have been, then, with enlightened civilians? This question I shall not answer; it was easy enough to see how it was with the Spanish ladies—they laughed, cheered, encored, clapped their hands, waved their handkerchiefs, and made every other sign which was characteristic of pleasure and delight. The contending brutes still strove together. Hercules quaked under the torturing hugs of Trojan. Trojan howled under the violent and painful perforations of Hercules. But the bear did not rely alone upon the efficacy of his arms; his massive jaws and formidable teeth were brought into service, and with them he inflicted deep wounds in his rival's flesh. He seized the bull between the ears and nostrils, and crushed the bones with such force that we could distinctly hear them crack! Nor were the stunning butts of the bull his only means of defence; his horns had been sharpened expressly for the occasion, and with these he lacerated the bear most frightfully. It was a mighty contest—a desperate struggle for victory!

Finally, however, fatigued, exhausted, writhing with pain and weltering in sweat and gore, they waived the quarrel and separated, as if by mutual consent. Neither was subdued; yet both felt a desire to suspend, for a time at least, all further hostilities. The bull, now exhausted and panting, cast a pacific glance towards the bear, and seemed to sue for an armistice; the bear, bleeding and languid after his furious contest, raised his eyes to the bull, and seemed to assent to the proposition. But, alas! man, cruel man, more brutal than the brutes themselves, would not permit them to carry out their pacific intentions. The two attendants or managers, Ignacio and Gomez, stepped up behind them, goading them with spears till they again rushed upon each other, and fought with renewed desperation. During this scuffle, the bull shattered the lower jaw of the bear, and we could see the shivered bones dangling from their bloody recesses! Oh, heaven! what a horrible sight. How the blood curdled in my veins. Pish! what a timid fellow I am, to allow myself to be agitated by such a trifle as this! Shall I tremble at what the ladies applaud? Forbid it, Mars! I'll be as spirited as they. But, to wind up this part of our story, neither the bear nor the bull could stand any longer—their limbs refused to support their bodies; they had worried and lacerated each other so much that their strength had completely failed, and they dropped upon the earth, gasping as if in the last agony. While in this helpless condition the chain was removed from their feet, horses were hitched to them, and they were dragged without the arena, there to end their miseries in death.

The second act of the afternoon's entertainment was now to be performed. It would be unnecessary, and painful to the feelings of sensitive readers, to dwell long upon this murderous sport. It was a mere repetition, in another form, of the disgusting horrors of that which preceded it. Fully satiated with the barbarities I had already witnessed, I am not sure that I should have staid to see any more, had it not been for the peculiar sensations which the cognomen of one of the actors awakened within me. By reference to the advertisement, it will be perceived that the two managers of this part of the proceedings were Joaquin Vatreto and Jesus Alvarez. The latter name sounded strangely in my ears. It occurred to me that it was peculiarly out of place in its present connection. What! Jesus at a bull-fight on Sunday, and not only at it, but one of the prime movers and abettors in it!

But now to the fight. All things being ready, the great bull, Behemoth, was freed from restraint, and sprang with frantic bounds into the midst of the arena. He bore a suitable appellation, for he was a monster in size and formidable in courage. Two picadors, Joaquin Vatreto and Jesus Alvarez, mounted on fiery steeds, with swords in hand, now entered and confronted him. Behemoth looked upon this sudden invasion as an intolerable insult. His territory was already too limited for so powerful a monarch as he considered himself, and he could not think of dividing it with others. The sight of these unceremonious intruders inflamed him with such rancor that he could no longer restrain himself; but lowering his head and tossing his tail aloft, he rushed furiously at them. They evaded his charge. The horses were well trained, and seemed to enjoy the sport, and to pride themselves upon their adroit manœuvres. But both they and their riders had enough to do to evade the fury of the enraged brute. Each successive bout became more animated and fierce. The foiling of the bull's purposes only exasperated him the more. There was not room enough in his capacious body to contain his effervescing wrath. The foam which he spurted from his mouth and nose fell upon the earth like enormous flakes of snow. Faster and faster, and with truer aim, he charged his foes. At last one of the horses, in attempting to wheel or turn suddenly round, stumbled, and the bull, taking advantage of the event, gored him so desperately in the abdomen that a part of his entrails protruded from the wounds and trailed almost upon the ground! This was truly a distressing scene. I could have wept for the poor, innocent charger, but in this case tears were of no avail.

One of the picadors now alighted, and engaged the attention of the bull, while the other led the two horses outside the inclosure. When this was done, a man on foot, called a matador, dressed in close-fitting, fantastic garments, with a heavy sword in his right hand, and a small red flag in his left, entered the arena and bowed first to the bull and then to the audience. It was now a matter of life and death between the bull and the matador. One or the other, or both, must die. If the bull did not kill the man, the man would kill the bull; if the man killed the bull, the man was to live, but if the bull killed the man, the bull was to die; so that death was sure to overtake the bull in any event. The action commenced, and waxed hotter and hotter every moment, and it was only by uncommon skill and agility that the matador could shun the frenzied charges of the bull. Had it not been for the flag which he carried in his hand, and which enabled him to deceive his antagonist by seeming to hold it directly before him, when in reality he inclined it to the right or to the left, as his safety dictated, the bull would unquestionably have dashed his brains out, thrown him over his head, or gored him to death. Nothing could have irritated or vexed the bull more than did the sight of this red flag, and he made all his assaults upon it, supposing, no doubt, that he would strike the mischief behind it, but the agile matador always took special care to spring aside and save himself from the deadly stroke. After tormenting, teasing and chafing him for about a quarter of an hour in this way, six keen javelins or darts, with miniature flags attached, were handed to the matador, who ventured to face the bull, and never quit him until he had planted them all in his shoulders, three in each. Stung to madness, the animal reared, rolled and plunged in the most frightful manner. Soon, however, he was on his feet again, pursuing his persecutor with renewed zeal.

The fates, however, were against him He could not comprehend, and consequently could not foil the crafty designs of his adversary, who completely deceived him with the flag. Night was now coming on, and it being time to close the performance, the matador, placing himself in a pompous attitude near the south side of the arena, challenged Behemoth to the last and decisive engagement by waving the flag briskly before him. The bull, exasperated beyond description, needed no additional incentive to urge him to meet the enemy. With a force apparently equal to that of a rhinoceros, and with the celerity of a reindeer, he rushed at the matador, who, stepping just sufficiently to the left to avoid him, thrust the sword into his breast up to the hilt. The matador, leaving this sword buried in the bull's body, now laid hold of another, which was on hand for the purpose, and stabbed him three times in a more vital part, when down he fell at his victor's feet, dead. Then jumping upon the carcass of his slain rival, the matador brandished his sword, doffed his hat, bowed his compliments, and retired, amid the deafening plaudits of a wolfish audience.

CHAPTER XI.

SACRAMENTO.

SACRAMENTO is situated on the river and in the heart of the valley of the same name, about one hundred miles north-east of San Francisco. It is the second city in the State in size, population and commerce, and contains from eight to ten thousand inhabitants—being nearly one fourth as large as San Francisco. It bears to San Francisco much the same relation that Columbia does to Charleston, or Albany to New York. From two to six steamboats daily ply between the two cities, conveying passengers and merchandise; and a vast deal of heavy freight is shipped in sailing vessels, which usually make the outward and return trip in a little over a week. The banks of the river are very low, and the current moves sluggishly towards the ocean. Flood-tide ascends almost as high as this place. The country, for twenty-five miles on either side of the river, is an unbroken plain, level as a floor, and would be invaluable for agricultural purposes were it not for the great freshets of the winter and spring, and the incessant drought of the summer and fall—two serious disadvantages to the farmer. Sometimes the whole valley is completely overflowed and remains under water for two or three consecutive months, on which occasions it presents the appearance of a vast lake. Many new immigrants, who are ignorant of the freaks of California seasons, arriving here in the summer, settle in this valley, and thank their stars that they were guided to an unclaimed plat of so much promise. But when winter comes and the windows of heaven are opened, and the river rises, and the cattle are drowned and the houses swept off, and they themselves compelled to fly to the upland to save their lives, they begin to discover the gloomy fact that they have been caught in a snare.

The site of the city, so smooth and flat, would be one of the most beautiful in the world, but for the lack of sufficient elevation. For the first two or three years after its settlement the inhabitants did nothing to protect it from the floods, but afterwards, becoming tired of navigating the streets in scows and skiffs, and willing to retain some of their goods and chattels about their premises, they built a temporary levee, which has since kept them tolerably dry. It is laid out with the most perfect regularity; its blocks and streets being as uniform and methodical as the squares of a chess-board. Those streets which run from north to south have alphabetical names, beginning with A, and ending with Z. Only four of them, I, J, K and L, are popular; the others command no business whatever, and but very few dwellings are situated on them. The cross-streets, or those which run from east to west, are designated arithmetically, commencing with 1st and continuing on in regular succession. Beyond 7th street, however, there are no buildings of any importance.

At present the legislature meets in this place; but as that august body is possessed of a remarkably roving disposition, having held its sessions at four different places within the last four years, at an extra expense to the State of nearly two hundred thousand dollars, it is yet uncertain whether this will be determined upon as the permanent capital. There is no capitol or state-house, nor is it likely that California will ever be able to build one while its finances are so recklessly managed. The receipts and expenditures of the State have, from the organization of its government to the present time, been intrusted to men who, to say nothing of their dishonesty, were as ignorant of the uses of money as a prodigal minor. Consequently they have entailed a public debt upon the people of more than three millions of dollars without effecting any general improvements excepting a marine hospital. This distinguished body, which now holds its deliberations in the court-house, contains some of the most precious scamps that ever paid devotion to the god of pelf; and, were it not that I have no wish to deal in personalities, I could here mention names which are notoriously infamous all over the Atlantic States. Are such men capable of devising measures for the public weal, or fit to enact laws for the commonwealth? Whether fit or unfit, they are about the only class of persons who are intrusted with the functions of legislation in this abominable land of concentrated rascality. The people of California, as a general thing, would as soon elect an honest, upright man to office, as Italian banditti would choose a moralist for their captain. No one here can be successful unless he assimilates himself to the people; he must carouse with villains, attend Sunday horse-races and bull-fights, and adapt himself to every species of depravity and dissipation.

Thus must a man discipline himself before he can receive the support and patronage of the public. It matters not what his occupation may be, whether merchant, mechanic, lawyer or doctor, he is sure to be ostracized, if he stands aloof from the vices and follies of the populace. Of course there are a few exceptions. Some men, thank heaven, have an innate abhorrence of every thing that savors of meanness or vulgarity, and they have nerve enough to cling to their principles at all times and in all places. No earthly power, even if backed by reinforcements from the infernal regions, could make them swerve from their fidelity to truth and justice. They have clearly defined ideas of right and wrong, and regulate their lives and conduct accordingly. They understand their duty, and endeavor to perform it. They see the evils of society, condemn and eschew them. There are a few such men in California, but they are discountenanced, neglected, sneered at, and flouted with opprobrious epithets. They are in bad odor; the majority is against them. The scoundrels are in power, and they have wrecked the country. Today the State is lawless, penniless and powerless. Such is the effect of the union of two bad things —a bad people and a bad country. It was necessary in the first place, to give even a passable character to the State, that the administration of affairs should have been committed to men of pre-eminent sagacity; but instead of pursuing this policy, the common interests have been confided to political charlatans, whose actions in every instance have been detrimental to the interests of the country. As a poor client suffers in the hands of a pettifogger, or as a patient laboring under an obscure and dangerous disease, sinks under the treatment of a quack, so has this poor, sick California suffered and sunk through the agency of her knavish managers.

Leaving these wire-pulling senators and hireling assemblymen, let us take a short stroll through one or two of the principal streets. We shall not observe any thing either curious or commendable in the styles of architecture. The houses are low, rarely exceeding two stories in height, and are built mostly of wood in the very cheapest manner. All the lumber used in their construction was brought from Oregon, first to San Francisco, and thence reshipped to this place. Here and there stands a plain but uncommonly stout and substantial brick store. I have never seen any buildings in the Atlantic States equal, in durability and security against fire, to the brick structures in California. They must build them so, for reasons heretofore given. Stone is not used at all; there is none in the vicinity.

As we wend our way through the town, we pass dozens of miserable, filthy little hotels, in any of which we can procure a bad meal for a dollar. A palatable dinner in one of the more respectable hotels will cost us twice that amount. We shall be considerably amused at the queer and unique canvas signs nailed over the doors of some of the dirty little huts and shanties around us. One of the taverns announces that it has "Tip-top Accommodations for Man and Beast;" at another we can find "Good Fare, and Plenty of it;" a third promises "Rest for the Weary and Storage for Trunks;" a fourth invites us to "Come in the Inn, and take a Bite;"

a fifth informs us that "Eating is done here;" a sixth assures us that "We have Rich Viands and Mellow Drinks;" while a seventh admonishes us to "Replenish the Stomach in our House." A bar, at which all kinds of liquors, raw and mixed, pure and sophisticated, are dealt out, is attached to each of these establishments; and it is generally a greater source of profit to the proprietor than the table. Small straw cots, with coarse blankets, which have never been submitted to any cleansing process, are provided for the guests to sleep on; and when they retire, they seldom remove any of their clothes, except their coats, and sometimes not even those. In the morning, when they rise to perform their ablutions, a single wash-pan answers for all, and one towel, redolent of a week's wiping, serves every guest.

More than two-thirds of the population of the northern part of the State lay in their supplies of provisions, clothing and mining implements at this place; and we shall notice several teams and pack-trains in the streets, loading and preparing to start on their journey. Mules and oxen are chiefly used, though for hauling short distances over good roads horses are employed. Some of the more remote mining districts, say two hundred miles from this place, are so rugged and mountainous that it is impossible to reach them with wagons or other vehicles, and the only means of transporting merchandise is upon the backs of mules. These hybrids, unamiable as is their appearance, are truly valuable for this purpose; they carry ponderous burdens, walk with ease upon the brink of a precipice, and can be kept in good serviceable condition by provender on which a horse would starve. After making a few trips they become very tractable, and it requires only four or five men to manage fifty or sixty of them. The packers have but little trouble with them, after strapping the loads on their backs and starting them off. They do not go abreast, but each follows closely behind another, Indian fashion; and they will travel patiently in this way from morning till night, rarely ever attempting a stampede.

Between the petty merchants who sell goods to those teamsters and muleteers, there is great rivalry and competition. I call them petty merchants because there are so many more of them than the business justifies or demands, that each one secures but a small share of the custom; and they have to resort to the most contemptible devices to pay current expenses. Indeed I do not believe half of them earn their support. The reader may think this strange, and wonder why men continue in an occupation which does not yield them a maintenance. They do not continue in it; their losses soon compel them to leave; but the departure of one victim only opens the way for the arrival of another. Their stands are immediately occupied by novices who, after the lapse of a few months, sink under the same fate that overwhelmed their luckless predecessors. Such is the routine of affairs all over the State. I have never known the time here when business was not clogged with double the number of traders it required. Ever since San Francisco and Sacramento were founded they have been overwhelmed with merchants, and this has been the case with every other city and town of any note throughout the State. In commercial circles you hear continual complaints of the dullness of the times. The merchants are always grumbling because they have nothing to do, and wondering when their business will improve. They live on the airy diet of hope; their good time is ever dancing before them, but never waits for them. It entices them on and then eludes them,—they reach after gold and find dross.

One reason why there is such an excess of business men, is, because American and European strangers, who have been led into the mistaken opinion that trading is profitable in California, are continually arriving with heavy stocks of goods, and opening new shops or going into the old ones, just vacated by those who could no longer sustain themselves under the pressure of the times. In this way the humbug is eternally nourished. As soon as one simpleton sacrifices his effects and retires, "a sadder and a wiser man," another fool steps in and takes his place. Question the New York, Baltimore and Boston shippers concerning the result of their ventures, and they will tell a doleful story. Ask the Liverpool, Bordeaux and Hamburg consignors to show the account sales of their factors, and they will anathematize the inquirer and California in the same breath. Now and then, it is true, when the markets are low, as they sometimes are, a shipment turns out lucrative beyond anticipation; but when such a thing occurs it is a mere matter of chance, and one gainful shipment occasions scores of unprofitable ones. Dependent as the State is upon importations for all that she consumes or requires for use, it must be expected that the markets will be very fluctuating and changeable,—at any rate, it is so. The price of any article does not remain the same two weeks at a time. There is almost always a superfluity of merchandise in market; the supply is generally double the demand, and many things are sold at less than prime cost. Yet, by the time this merchandise falls into the hands of the actual consumer, it usually costs him from one to four hundred per cent. more than he would have to pay for it in the Atlantic States. The consignee will probably sell it to a speculator—the speculator to a wholesale merchant—the wholesale merchant to a jobber—the jobber to a retailer—the retailer to a muleteer, and the muleteer to the final purchaser or consumer. Or the importer may sell it to the city grocer, whose onerous rent makes it necessary for him to re-sell at an extraordinary advance on invoice rates to defray expenses. Thus the charges accruing on it, after its arrival, render it very costly.

I might cite instances of the perfidy and dishonesty of California merchants; but it would be like taking an inventory of the exact number of blades of grass in a meadow in order to get at the weeds by subtraction,—it would be easier to reverse the task. It would require less time to tell of those who have been true to their trusts. I know one man in San Francisco who received a consignment of nearly twelve thousand dollars worth of merchandise from his brother in New York. He placed it in an auction house—had it sold for what it would bring—appropriated the proceeds to his own use, and wrote back to his brother that all the goods had been destroyed by fire. His brother heard of his unfaithfulness, came on to San Francisco and reasoned with him; but could neither bring him to terms nor find law that would compel the performance of a common obligation. The defrauded brother returned home without recovering a cent of his dues. Another New Yorker consigned twenty thousand dollars' worth of merchandise to two different commission houses (ten thousand to each,) with limited instructions—that is, not to sell for less than a certain sum. The factors received the goods, hurried them through the market, put the funds in their pockets, and wrote to the consignor, informing him that his ventures had been consumed by fire, and sympathizing with him in his losses! Before long, however, the shipper was made acquainted with the villainy of his agents, and applied to the courts for redress; but this was only employing a rogue to catch a rogue. After a deal of expense and delay, the case was dismissed. A whole cargo of wares and merchandise, valued at a trifle less than three hundred thousand dollars, was intrusted to another man, who disposed of it and absconded with the money.

But why detail these swindling transactions? Volumes upon volumes might be filled with accounts of the crimes and short-comings of this wretched country; but their perusal would only be productive of abhorrence and disgust. If, reader, you would know California, you must go live there. It is impossible for me to give, or for you to receive a correct impression of it on paper,—like Thomas, the unbelieving disciple, you must *see* and *feel* before you can be convinced.

On the night of the 2d of November, 1852, Sacramento was almost entirely destroyed by fire. Twenty-two hundred buildings, with other property, valued at ten millions of dollars, were completely reduced to ashes. The wind was blowing very hard at the time the fire commenced, and the roaring of the flames, the rapidity with which they spread, the explosions of gunpowder, as house after house was blown up, formed a scene rarely excelled in terrific grandeur. Men, women and children ran to and fro in the greatest confusion, excited almost to frenzy, in the effort to save their lives and effects. Within six hours after the fire first broke out, more than nine-tenths of the city were swept into oblivion, and the people were left to sleep on the naked earth without any shelter but the clothing they had on. Happening, too, just at the commencement of the rainy season, this conflagration was peculiarly disastrous, as thousands were deprived not only of shelter, but also of the means of securing a comfortable living. Provisions at the time were scarcer than I ever knew them before, or have known them since; and the extraordinarily high prices which they commanded almost precluded the poorer classes from buying or using them at all. Flour sold at forty-two dollars per barrel, pork at fifty-five, and other eatables in about the same ratio. Farther in the interior the times were still harder. In some of the distant mining localities flour and pork sold as high as three dollars per pound—equal to five hundred and eighty-eight dollars per barrel; and could not be had in sufficient quantities even at these rates.

Many then suffered the pangs of insatiable hunger; and I have seen children crying to their parents for bread, when there was none to give them.

A California conflagration is a scene of the most awful grandeur that the mind is capable of conceiving. When fire is once communicated to the buildings, especially if it be in the dry season, when the winds rage and every thing is crisped by the sun, it does not smoulder, but blazing high in the air, and spreading far and wide, it consumes every thing within its reach, and leaves nothing behind but cinders and desolation. No one of the present day, out of California, has ever seen such pyramids of flame. One of the most beautiful sights I ever beheld was during a large fire in San Francisco. It was a moonless night, and there was nothing visible in the dark concave of heaven, save a few twinkling stars. Others were concealed by the detached masses of floating vapor which obscured them. Soon after the conflagration commenced, the brilliant illumination attracted large flocks of brant from the neighboring marshes; and as they flew hither and thither, high over the flaming element, they shone and glistened as if they had been winged balls of fire darting through the air. Had their plumage been burnished gold, they could not have been more radiant.

Before taking our final leave of Sacramento,

we must not fail to get a glimpse of the Three Cent Philosopher, a Mormon polygamist, who figures conspicuously in this city as an extortionate usurer. He was born in the State of New York, near the hallowed spot where Jo Smith received his apostolic diploma. The Three Cent Philosopher does not carry so small a purse as his common appellation might seem to indicate; he is the wealthiest man in the place, and is as tenacious of his property as of his life. It is supposed that he is worth very near half a million of dollars. Though he believes in polygamy, and practices it, yet he never lives with more than one spouse at a time; to have them all around him at once would be too expensive.

When his wife goes out shopping he gives her fifty cents, and if she happens to bring back one-tenth of the amount, he takes it from her and locks it up in his safe. When he travels on a steamboat he always takes deck passage, and carries food in his pockets to avoid the extra expense of dining at the table. While passing through the streets he keeps a vigilant lookout for stray nails, old horse-shoes, pieces of bagging and other refuse, which he picks up, lugs home and deposits in his repository of odds and ends. Instead of chairs, he sits on stools and boxes of his own make; and, in place of coffee, he drinks parched barley tea or watered milk. His disposition is quite as sweet as wormwood, and his household is usually a scene of as much calm and domestic bliss as a family of tomcats. He is in the habit of bickering with his family at least once every day, and when he does so he rouses the whole neighborhood with the noise of his oaths and imprecations. In all probability he is a lineal descendant of Ishmael, the son of Hagar, for his hand is against every man and every man's hand is against him. He is at enmity with all the world and is despised by every body. If his neighbor looks at him, he curses him, and if an acquaintance says good-morning to him, he tells him to go to h—ll. He has never been known to entertain a charitable thought towards his fellow-men, nor to speak a good word concerning his nearest relations. To sum up all, he is the extract of ill-breeding, the essence of vulgarity, and the quintessence of meanness.

CHAPTER XII.

YUBA—THE MINER'S TENT.

My first experience in mining was obtained on the banks of the Yuba river, a small tributary of the Feather, which is itself a branch of the Sacramento. Our party, in a stage-coach, left Sacramento city early in the morning; we traveled due north until late in the afternoon, when we arrived at Marysville, a city containing eight or nine thousand inhabitants, and situated at the confluence of the Yuba and Feather rivers. It was in July, and the roads were four to six inches deep in dust, which seemed to be as fine as bolted flour, and was so volatile that it rose in a dense cloud as we passed through it. The heat of the sun was oppressive in the extreme, and by the time we got to the place mentioned above, our persons were so besmeared with dust and perspiration that it was no easy matter for a stranger to determine our natural color.

I could have made the trip by water, as there is steamboat communication between Sacramento and Marysville daily; but having sailed up the river as high as this place once before on a pleasure excursion, I preferred the land route for the sake of seeing the country. I was disappointed, however; for, as the distance between the two cities is a mere continuation of the Sacramento valley, I saw nothing materially different from the purlieus of the city I had left. The surface of the valley is remarkably level, and is sparsely timbered with scrubby oaks and other gnarled trees of uncommon form. Nor is there any thing of unusual interest to be seen in Marysville. Sacramento is its prototype, and it has been modeled after that city with scrupulous exactness. I never saw two places more alike.

By means of the same conveyance that carried us to Marysville, we resumed our northern journey early in the morning of the succeeding day, and by twelve o'clock we reached the place of our destination. We were now on Long Bar, a popular mining place, divided and watered by the Yuba. Two miles beyond is Park's Bar, which I had visited on a previous occasion; but this was the first time I had ever entered the mines for the purpose of digging gold. Now, however, I had come to try my luck, and to see what the gnomes and fairies would do for me.

Once fairly started in a miner's life, I could not completely steel myself against the extravagant hopes which seemed to float in the very atmosphere of the mines. Wild and extravagant fancies would in spite of me obtrude themselves upon what I thought a well-balanced mind. Nor were these reveries by any means unnatural, unreasonable though they might be. Thousands of miners have, from time to time, indulged hopes equally impalpable and transitory. I was standing over deposits of gold, and who could tell how large they were, or how easily they might be found? Who knew but that I should dig from these hills more wealth than was ever locked up in the vaults of the Rothschilds?

I had supplied myself with abundance of provisions, a pair of good blankets, and every needful mining implement. Being in what is called surface diggings, that is, on a spot where the gold lies near the surface of the earth, I could perform all the necessary manipulations myself. I noticed that those around did not delve deeper than from three to four feet in this place. It did not pay to go lower; and whether it paid to dig at all, will be seen hereafter. My implements consisted of a pick, a spade, a pan, a bucket, a cradle and a wheelbarrow. The *cradle*, though rudely made and of rude material, was a very good one, and I have since regretted that I did not keep it and bring it with me, as it would have answered a domestic purpose quite as well as a more costly one. The modus operandi of single-handed mining may be described in a few words. The earth is loosened with the pick, thrown into the wheelbarrow with the spade, rolled to the river, emptied into the cradle, washed by pouring water over it from the bucket, and carefully rocked until the gold is separated from the dirt. The clods of earth, during this process of washing, slowly dissolve, or are suspended in the water, whereupon the gold, (if there is any,) being heaviest, sinks to the bottom. All the contents of the cradle are then turned out, except a thin layer at the bottom, which is supposed to contain the precious metal. The next and last process is to scoop this layer into the pan, and wash and rewash it until the dirt is entirely separated from the gold. A sieve, or rather a piece of punctured or perforated sheet-iron, which catches the larger stones and other insoluble substances, is fixed about midway the depth of the cradle. The gold is generally found in small particles about the size of grains of sand, sometimes not half so large, sometimes much larger. The size of the grains, as well as the quantity, depends very much upon the locality. No lumps larger than a small pea were obtained from this bar.

Fearing that I might make a fortune immediately, and return to the city without learning how the gold gleaners live, I determined not to commence operations until I had scrutinized the whole bar, tents, miners, mining and all. Indeed it was necessary for me to converse with some of the miners, in order to acquaint myself with their laws respecting claims, dams and water. All surface diggings, when marked out, or laid off in small plats, are called bars; and these bars are known by distinctive names, as, for instance, Rocky Bar, Steep Bar, Sandy Bar, &c. The name is not always derived from a peculiarity of the place. Frequently they are called by the names of the men who first discovered gold on them, as Brown's Bar, Hall's Bar, Drake's Bar; and sometimes they take their names from an important event that occurred at or near them at the time they were opened, as Highwayman's Bar, Rioter's Bar, Murderer's Bar. Among the more fanciful names that designate localities in various parts of the mines are the following: Whiskey Bar, Humbug Creek, One Horse Town, Mississippi Quarters, Mad Ox Ravine, Mad Mule Canon, Skunk Flat, Woodpecker Hill, Jesus Maria, Yankee Jim's Diggings, Death Pass, Ignis Fatuus Placer, Devil's Retreat, Bloody Bend, Jackass Gulch, Hell's Half Acre.

Every Bar is governed by such laws as the majority of the miners see fit to enact, not by written or published documents, but by verbal understanding. All the mines are public property, that is, they belong to the United States government, which, in its suicidal liberality, exercises comparatively no jurisdiction over them. So far as the general government is concerned, Chinese marauders and foreign cut-throats have the same rights and privileges guaranteed to them, in this matter, as American citizens. Besides the enormous sums of money that the federal government paid for California, it did a great deal of hard fighting, and now has to keep a body of troops stationed there to prevent the Indians from desolating the country; but aliens, who bear no part of the burden, and who refuse to become permanent settlers or citizens, are permitted, nay, encouraged, to come in on an equal footing. No tax is levied upon them. They are protected from the Indians by our soldiery, and share all the benefits with the native citizens; yet they are not required to aid in defraying the common expenses. It can hardly be doubted that this is bad policy? Would it not be bad management in a father, after having bought a farm, to let strangers come in and carry off the fruits of the soil, to the detriment and impoverishment of his own children? If so, then our government, as a general mother, is doubly culpable.

Almost every Bar is governed by a different code of laws, and the sizes of the claims vary according to locality. In one place a man may hold twice, thrice, or even quadruple the number of feet that are allowed him in another. One fourth of an acre is an average-sized claim. The discoverer of new diggings is awarded a double or triple share, or only an equal part, as a majority of those on the ground shall determine. Two claims cannot be held by one person at the same time, except by purchase. If a man lets his claim go unworked a certain number of days, say five, eight or ten, he forfeits it, and any other person is at liberty to take possession of it. When a miner wishes to quit his claim only for a few days, he stacks his tools upon it, notifies two or three adjoining neighbors of his intention, and goes where he pleases. If he returns within the time prescribed by the laws of the Bar, he is entitled to resume his claim; but if he is absent a day longer, it falls to the first person, without a claim, who may happen to find it. There is more real honesty and fairness among the miners than any other class of people in California. Taken as a body, they are a plain, straight-forward, hard-working set of men, who attend to their own business without meddling in the affairs of others; and I have found as guileless hearts amongst them as ever throbbed in mortal bosom. Genuine magnanimity or nobleness of soul, when found at all in California, must be sought among the miners—especially among those who are farthest removed from the contaminating influences of idlers and gamblers.

Drones and sluggards—things in the shape of men, who are too lazy to work for an honest living—are the chief authors of the horrible crimes that have rendered this country so odious and despicable. They are the persons who are always creating disturbances; cheating, robbing and murdering; and there is such a legion of them that no place is exempt from their presence. Wherever there is money they may be seen skulking around it; and if they cannot filch it from the rightful owner by intrigue or artifice, they will do it by more violent measures. They lurk behind the poor drudging miner, even in the farthest gorges of the mountains, and there butcher him, that they may avail themselves of his hard-earned treasures. An incident of this nature, which terminated most admirably, occurred near this place but a few days before my arrival. A highwayman met a miner in an unfrequented place, and, with a cocked pistol pointing towards him, demanded, "Your gold this instant, sir, or your life!" "Hold! you shall have it," exclaimed the miner, when quickly thrusting his hand into his breast pocket, as if feeling for his purse, he drew his own revolver and shot the would-be assassin dead upon the spot.

While reconnoitering the bar, I made excuses to call on several miners who happened to be in their tents. As for the tents themselves, though nearly all of the same size, they differ very much in appearance and quality. A great many are made of duck or white canvas; while others are built of stunted saplings, which grow sparsely throughout the mining region. Those constructed of the latter material are about the size and shape of a common hog-pen, with a stick and mud chimney, which very frequently has a headless whiskey barrel stuck in the top for a funnel. These are the best and most comfortable domicils about the mines; and it is only when miners, or a combination of miners, have large claims, which afford them steady employment for a considerable length of time, that they are enabled to build them. There being no planks, boards, slabs, nor other sawn or hewn timbers, the poles are covered with brush or coarse cloth, and sometimes with raw-hides. The ground is the floor in all cases. No chimney nor whiskey-barrel flue graces the gable-end of the canvas tent; it is merely a temporary shelter from the scorching rays of the sun and the chilling dews of the night. Until the miner is successful enough to secure a good claim and build himself a hovel, of course he is compelled to sleep under the roof which canopied Adam and Eve, and he must take his chances of the tarantula and of the assassin.

The interior of the miner's tent corresponds to its exterior. Spread upon the ground, on one side, we see a pair of rumpled blankets, upon which he sleeps. They are thoroughly saturated with mud and dust, and have never been shaken, switched nor sunned since their place was assigned them. Scattered here and there, about the edges of the blankets, lie several of Paul de Kock's and Eugene Sue's yellow-backed novels, whose soiled margins and dog-eared leaves give evidence that they are not allowed to go unread. Something less than half a dozen packs of cards are within reach, while three or four old stumps or chunks of wood, employed as substitutes for chairs, occupy random positions about the floor. In one corner is a keg of brandy or whiskey, and in another the cooking apparatus and provisions. As for tables, delft-ware, knives and forks, or any thing of that kind, there are none. The miner always carries his pistol and bowie knife by his side day and night, and with the latter weapon, aided by his fingers, he reduces his food to convenient morsels.

His cooking utensils consist of a frying-pan and a pot, neither of which, except in rare instances, is ever washed. The pot is mostly used for boiling pork and beans, and the old scum and scales that accumulate on the inside from one ebullition serve as seasoning to the next. Pork and beans are two of the principal articles of diet with miners, partly because they are comparatively cheaper than other provisions, and partly on account of their being so nutritious and wholesome. The beans, especially, are very fine; they are imported from Chili, and are superior to any I ever saw in the Atlantic States. By boiling as much at one time as the pot will hold, the miner generally saves himself the trouble of preparing these articles of food oftener than twice a week. When cooked to suit him, he sets the pot on one side, leaving the contents in it uncovered; this is his pantry, and out of it he makes his meals from time to time, until all is consumed, when he replenishes it with a fresh supply of the same kind. Flap-jacks are very frequently used in lieu of bread. They are a combination of flour and water, fried in such grease as can be extracted from the pork; or, if the miner has no pork, he bakes them as he would other thin cakes of dough. If he is not too far removed from a depot of general provisions, he will probably keep a bottle of molasses, which may be seen by the side of the frying-pan, unstopped, and containing an amount of flies and ants nearly equal to that of the saccharine juice. These entrapped insects do not seem to come within the scope of his observation, as he never attempts to clear his bottle of them. He is not very squeamish about his diet.

It is but seldom that the miner suspends labor on Sunday if his claim is a rich one; but if it is poor, he usually lets it rest on that day, while he does his washing and mending. I have already said that he carries his bowie-knife and revolver with him day and night. There is scarcely an exception to this rule; ninety-nine out of every hundred are thus armed, and this accounts for the fatal result of almost every altercation. No matter what it is that occasions disputes between men, whether slight misunderstandings or grave difficulties, few words are bandied before they appeal to their weapons, and the life of one or the other is sure to be lost in the fracas,—sometimes both are killed. This barbarous practice of carrying deadly weapons is not alone confined to the miners; you rarely find a merchant, mechanic, lawyer doctor, or man of any other calling in California, who does not keep them concealed about him. By a calculation, based upon fair estimates, I learn that since California opened her mines to the world, she has invested upwards of six millions of dollars in bowie-knives and pistols—pretty playthings to give to her children!

Having surveyed and examined the bar, and all that pertained to it, to my satisfaction, I constructed a small canvas tent, and the next day began to search the earth in quest of gold. Though I was not reared in idleness, this was my first lesson in real hard labor. Here, in the summer season, the thermometer ranging from 90 to 105 degrees of Fahrenheit in the shade, mining, when diligently and assiduously prosecuted, is certainly the most toilsome employment in the world. I imagine that the tillage of sugar-fields is pastime compared with it, and that the African slaves who gather coffee in Brazil, have no adequate conception of hard-work.

For three months I applied myself to my tools and claim with all the energy of my nature—digging, shoveling and rocking, with the snarls of grizzly bears to lull me to sleep at night, and the howls of hungry wolves to regale my ears at the break of day. With all this wear and tear of body and mind, my account-current of proceeds and expenditures stood, at the expiration of that time, giving myself no credit for either loss of time or physical exhaustion, just ninety-three and three-quarter cents — balance on hand! This was building a palace with a vengeance! A net profit of ninety-three and a quarter cents in three months, being "two and sixpence" per month, or a fraction over a cent a day.

Hope, however, did not forsake me, and besides that, (shall I confess it?) I felt a sort of malignant satisfaction that I was not alone in my disappointments. I found consolation in the misfortune of others! When I looked around me, and saw scores of dirty, hungry, ragged, long-haired miners, who had toiled and labored like plantation negroes, on this and other bars, for more than two years, and who could not command as much as five dollars to save their lives, it buoyed me up, and made me better satisfied with my own ill-luck. The feeling that thus manifested itself may have been worthy of censure, but I am sure it was natural, for no energetic or enterprising man likes to see his neighbor out-do him, or surpass him in the acquisition of wealth—especially if their chances and opportunities have always been the same. If I had not been unsuccessful myself, I should not have chuckled over the corresponding misfortunes of others; but, to be candid, feeling that my devotion and application to business entitled me to a reasonable share of prosperity, I had but little sympathy for my fellow-miners, who, being no more worthy of reward than myself, failed in their efforts to excel me. I said I had but little sympathy for them. I had some. It grieved me to see so many stout, athletic men undergoing so many privations and discomforts, wasting their time in unprofitable schemes, only to be at last subjected to the most galling disappointments.

The time had now come, however, for other thoughts and considerations. A change of location seemed to be necessary. The profits of mining did not warrant longer continuance at this place. It occurred to me that the sum of ninety-three and three-quarter cents was but indifferent remuneration for three months' herculean labor. I wished to have nothing to do with this lying equivalent, so handing it over, with my compliments, to a poor, needy, hungry-looking neighbor, I shook the dust from my feet and departed, after the manner of Lot when he left Sodom, not deigning to look behind—not for fear, however, of being turned into a pillar of gold.

CHAPTER XIII.

STOCKTON AND SONORA.

I HAVE perambulated the streets of San Francisco, Sacramento, Marysville and Stockton; but of all the California cities, after San Francisco, Stockton is my choice. It is named in honor of Commodore R. F. Stockton, and is situated on a tributary of the San Joaquin river, which empties into the Suisun Bay, opening into the Bay of San Francisco. Being but a little over one hundred miles to the east of San Francisco, it enjoys the advantages of daily steamboat communication with that place; but owing to the narrow banks of the stream and the shallowness of the water, the vessels are much smaller than those employed upon the Sacramento. It contains from six to seven thousand inhabitants. Though only the fourth city in the State in population, it is the third in business. All the residents of the southern mines draw their supplies from it; and as it is blessed with a mild climate, it is frequently resorted to by those who seek pastime or recreation.

The San Joaquin valley, in the midst of which this city is situated, would probably be the best agricultural land in the State, if the water could be drained from it; but in its present low and boggy condition, it is utterly unfit for cultivation. It takes its name from the low-banked river which meanders through it, and is as level as a garden. No vegetable production is found upon it, except the tule, a tall, pithy species of rush or calamus, which bears a more striking resemblance to the flag than to any thing else of Atlantic growth. This tule, which grows as thick as it can stand, and from six to eight feet in height, is an annual plant; and in the fall of the year, if fire be communicated to it during the night, when there is a light breeze stirring, it burns with an indescribable splendor. I have said that this aquatic weed is the only natural product of the valley; this is true, as regards all that part which is perfectly level, and which presents the appearance of a vast meadow; but as we approach the Coast Range on the south-west, or the Sierra Nevadas on the north-east, we come to slightly elevated knolls, upon which we find clumps of gnarled oaks. These trees all lean towards the east, as if bowing their heads in adoration, having grown in this reverential posture while under the influence of the winds from the west.

This valley affords another evidence of the unfavorable condition of the country. It shows conclusively that even the most valuable parts of the State are encumbered with insurmountable impediments. The bottom lands, which are mainly relied upon for agricultural purposes, are too wet to till, and too low to drain; while the uplands are so dry and sterile that neither grains, plants nor fruits can be raised upon them. There is either too much moisture or none at all. It is a land of mountains and mud-holes. Still, there are some extensive plains and valleys which might be successfully cultivated, if the seasons were adapted to them; but the absence of rain during the summer renders them of little or no value to the farmer. It is very probable, however, that in the progress of time, as the other members of the confederacy become burdened with population, the more eligible parts of this State will be settled and, by means of irrigation, made tolerably productive; but when California is thus peopled and converted into a place of permanent habitation, it will be by the force of destiny, rather than by any attractions it can offer to immigrants. They may make it their home as a dernier resort, but they will not do it as a matter of choice. So long as there is any unappropriated territory in other parts of the Union, California will not be in demand.

We shall find but few things deserving attention in the city of Stockton, having already examined its archetypes, San Francisco and Sacramento. It is due to this place to remark that,

notwithstanding all its Peter Funk and Cheap John establishments, it sustains a better character than any other city in the State. Though it has its share of groggeries and gambling-houses, and is, in most respects, fitted out in true California style, it is not infested with so many drones and desperadoes as are usually met with in neighboring towns. I am well aquainted with many of its citizens and know them to be estimable men—not too lazy to work, nor too sour to laugh at a merry thing.

Sonora is an inland town, situated in the midst of one of the richest mineral regions in the southern part of the State. A stage-coach affords the most convenient and expeditious means of reaching this place, which lies about fifty miles to the south-east. Starting early in the morning, we travel as fast as a dare-devil driver can make four horses convey us—frequently meeting and overtaking numerous pack trains, pedestrians and ox-teams, passing to and fro between the mines and Stockton. A part of the country over which our road leads us, is a somewhat elevated plain, which, being entirely destitute of trees and other vegetable products, presents a most dreary and uninviting prospect. We see nothing around us but the naked earth. There is no accommodation for either bird or beast—no resting-place for the one, nor food for the other. The pack-trains, pedestrians and ox-

teams, constitute the only animal life in view; and as we see them plodding along over this barren waste, our memories are refreshed with vivid recollections of those stories, which we read in former days, of caravans crossing the great desert of Sahara.

It is a fact worthy of being here recorded, as illustrative of the success of the miners, that we shall observe a larger number returning on foot than we find going. I was amused one day, while on my way to the regions of hidden treasure, when meeting a ragged, hairy, Esau-looking pedestrian, he hailed me with "Hallo." "How are you?" answered I. "Which way?" asked he. "To the mines," replied I. "Well, my friend," said he, "you will excuse me for speaking plainly; this is a free country and I presume you are at liberty to go to the mines or to the d—l, just as you please; but, mark my words, if you are going to the mines to dig, I'll be d—d if you don't rue the act." "May-be not," remarked I. "Very well," he added, "you'll see. By the time you delve and toil two long years, under the broiling sun as I have done, and have seen others do, without making a decent living, you'll perceive the truth of what I tell you."

Steadily pursuing our course, about twelve o'clock we came to the Stanislaus River, a small tributary stream of the San Joaquin. Here we stop to change horses and get dinner, there being a sort of bastard hotel near the brink of the river. Numerous Indians, naked and hungry, could be seen prowling about this place, or seated in squads, partaking of a mess of worms, young wasps, grasshoppers, or any other similar dainty to which their good stars may lead them. It was a long time before the savage creatures would tolerate the presence of the white man amongst them; but they have been so repeatedly routed in battle, that they have now given up open hostility and are comparatively peaceable; still they secretly cherish the most implacable enmity to our race, and improve every opportunity to dispatch us when they can do so without being detected. They gain nothing, however, by these covert misdeeds; for our people, understanding their insidious conduct, retaliate by deliberately shooting them down whenever they come in their way. What the white man's life is valued at by the Indian, is probably not known; but the white man hurls the Indian into eternity with as much nonchalance as though he were a squirrel.

Having appeased our appetites and secured the services of a fresh team, we cross the river and resume our journey. As we advance towards the place of our destination, the face of the country changes, from level plains to rugged slopes and woodlands. In the forenoon our road, though disagreeably dusty, was both smooth and straight, but now it winds over rocky glades, hills and gullies; and as the wheels of our vehicle mount and descend the rough impediments, we are jarred and shaken without mercy. Approaching still nearer the end of our journey, we have to contend with a more difficult and uneven surface; but being in charge of a very skillful driver, we are drawn safely over every rock and crag.

Arriving in Sonora between sundown and dark, we repair to a public house, and bespeak supper and lodgings for the night. The best hotel in the place is a one-story structure, built of unhewn saplings, covered with canvas and floored with dirt. It consists of one undivided room, in which the tables, berths and benches are all arranged. Here we sleep, eat and drink. Four or five tiers of berths or bunks, one directly above another, are built against the walls of the cabin, by means of upright posts and cross-pieces, fastened with thongs of raw-hide The bedding is composed of a small straw mattress about two feet wide, an uncased pillow stuffed with the same material, and a single blanket. When we creep into one of these nests, it is optional with us whether we unboot or uncoat ourselves; but it would be looked upon as an act of ill-breeding, even in California, to go to bed with one's hat on. Having once resigned ourselves into the arms of Morpheus, we are not likely to be disturbed by the drunken yells and vociferations of night-brawlers, now that we have become accustomed to such things. The noisy curses of the rabble will have no more effect upon us than the roaring water-fall or the mill-wheel has upon the miller. Night glides away, morning dawns, and we rise from our bunks to battle with another day. On the outside of the tavern, whither we betake ourselves to wash, are a tub of water, a basin and a towel, for all the guests; but as only one person can perform his ablutions at a time, it will be necessary for us to form ourselves in a line, and take our turn—the first comers being entitled to the front places. We are now ready to replenish the inner man. The bar is convenient for those who wish to imbibe. Breakfast is announced. We seat ourselves at the table. Before us is a reasonable quantity of beans, pork and flapjacks, served up in tin plates. Pea tea, which the landlord calls coffee with a bold emphasis, is handed to us, and we help ourselves to such other things as may be within reach.

No matter what kinds or qualities of viands are set before us, so that there be sufficient, for our stomachs have become so well tempered by this time that we feast upon them with as much gusto as if we were dining in a French restaurant. Neither spices, sauces nor seasonings are necessary to accommodate them to the palate. Our appetites need no nursing. Honest hunger disdains such dyspeptic accompaniments as the contents of cruets and casters. The richest condiments are the poorest provisions.

Our fast is broken—we are satisfied. The proprietor of the hotel, with his two male assistants, begins to clear off the table. Women have no hand in these domestic affairs. There is not a female about the establishment. All the guests, owners and employees are men. The dishes are washed, the blankets straightened in the berths; and while the cook is preparing dinner, some of the tavern-loungers seat themselves around the table, to take a friendly game of euchre, whist, seven-up, laugh-and-lay-down, old-maid, commerce or matrimony, while others saunter off to the gambling houses, of which there are about half a dozen in the place, to play at roulette, monte, faro, poker, twenty-one, all-fours or lansquenet. Such is hotel life in California, especially in the country towns and throughout the mining region.

Frequently several of the guests are fuddled, and as there are no partitions or apartments in the building, by which one person or set of persons may be separated from another, they are a most prolific source of annoyance to their sober neighbors. I recollect one occasion particularly, when, fatigued by a long day's journey, I stopped at one of these mountain taverns in the hope of enjoying a comfortable night's rest. Soon after eating my supper, which consisted of the standard dish, pork and beans, I crept into one of the farthest bunks, annoyed by the blackguardism and segar fumes of a group of drunken card-players, who occupied a table near the centre of the room. These swaggering inebriates, noisy as they were, did not prevent me from sleeping, as I had become habituated to witnessing such nocturnal carousals; but towards midnight, in came a wild, blustering lunatic, who had lost his reason about a week before, yelling and screaming as if a legion of fiends were after him. He was bare-footed, bare-headed and bare-legged, having no clothing upon his person, except a shirt; and I understood afterwards that he had been roaming about the place four or five days and nights in this condition. Making some inquiry concerning his history, I learned that he was a lawyer by profession, that he had formerly figured as an able and influential member of the Maine Legislature, and that, becoming embarrassed in his financial affairs, he left his family and emigrated hither in the hope of retrieving his fortune. Shortly after his arrival, not finding employment for his talent as a counselor, he determined to seek the favor of the mines; but his efforts in that quarter proved unavailing. For nearly a year he had toiled vigorously and incessantly, but to no purpose. He could not discover the hidden treasure which he sought.

Disappointed and chagrined at the result, he resigned himself to the bottle. The remembrance of his dependent and far distant family, coupled with the mischievous influence of ardent spirits, increased and sharpened his mental suffering; his mind began to vacillate—his reason lost its equilibrium, and we now find him a raving maniac. More than half naked, friendless and forlorn, he wanders about the streets and through the woods, day and night — a poor, miserable, crazy vagabond. Why, it may be asked, was there not some public provision made for the removal and security of this pitiable nuisance? Simply because it was in California. Here, where there is nothing as it should be, this unhappy man was allowed to run at large. No one cared for him. He was supposed to be harmless, and was, therefore, permitted to live. If he had inflicted any bodily injury upon any one, he would probably have been shot or stabbed, and that would have been the end of the drama. Cases of this or a similar character are to be met with almost every day. I only mention this as a single instance.

To give a faint idea of the precocity and waywardness of youth in this country, I will relate a bloody incident which occurred at another hotel, where I had put up for a night's lodging. In this case the landlord, a short, lean Massachusetts Yankee, was married and had his family with him. His eldest son, Ned, had not seen his ninth year. Nevertheless, this boy had learned to gamble. Whether his father or mother had instructed him in the art, or whether he had been tutored by the blacklegs frequenting the hotel, I am unable to say; but it was very evident that his parents cared very little about the matter, for they permitted him to play cards in their own house, and seemed to pride themselves upon his proficiency. Indeed, he was so dexterous in his manner of shuffling and dealing, and so quick to perceive the course and probable result of the game, that he was known throughout the neighborhood as the gambling prodigy. It may be questioned whether Hoyle himself was so conversant with diamonds, hearts, clubs and spades at so early an age.

Supper was now over, and the tables were surrounded with players. Little Ned had his place amongst them. I watched him more than an hour. He handled the cards with so much grace, skill and agility, and seemed to be so perfectly familiar with every branch of the game, that I could not withhold my admiration. As the night advanced, the parties became involved in a quarrel. Some one accused Ned of unfairness in changing the position of certain cards. Violent oaths and maledictions followed this accusation. Inflamed with anger, and assuming a menacing attitude, Ned denounced his accuser (a full grown man, three times as large and four times as old as himself,) as "a pusillanimous liar and scoundrel," and added, "G–d d—n you, I'll shoot you!" By this time the excitement had reached a high pitch. Things began to wear an alarming aspect. Several persons took sides in the matter, some for Ned and some against him. A general row seemed to be inevitable. Ned had the largest number of friends; but his enemies were clamorous and obstinate in their assertions that he had departed from the rules of the game, and declared in positive terms that he was a disciplined cheat.

Finally, however, Ned's friends took upon themselves all the responsibility of his behaviour, and the war of loud invectives and imprecations was now waged more by the adherents of the original disputants than by those disputants themselves. The bandying of gross epithets attracted the attention of a large crowd. Serious consequences were apprehended. The occasion was pregnant with mischief. One of the desperadoes jerked a bowie-knife from his pocket, and was about to plunge it into the body of his antagonist, when another drew a revolver and shot him. A few struggles—a few groans, and the fallen man had ceased to live. But the injury was not confined to him alone. As the ball passed through the breast of the man at whom it was aimed, it lodged in the shoulder of an in-

15*

nocent spectator, inflicting a severe but not mortal wound. And now was enacted one of those awful scenes of retribution for which California is so notorious. The man who had just committed the homicide was seized by the mob, and, amid loud cries of "hang him! hang him!" led out to a tree and there summarily executed according to the prompt sentence of the excited multitude. It was a season of dreadful uproar and commotion. The man who was shot had not been dead half an hour before his murderer was suspended by the neck between heaven and earth. Thus we have seen the blood of two men shed in the quarrel of a stripling, who had not attained half the age of manhood, but who already was a reckless and abandoned little gambler. If we deemed it necessary, we might cite other instances of a similar character. Suffice it to say that this boy, Ned, may be taken as a fair sample of the rising generation in California. Of course, they are not all exactly like him, any more than two persons are exactly alike any where else; but the same unlimited freedom is extended to them all; they are allowed to do just as they please. What else can be expected? Is it to be supposed that parents who put no restraint upon themselves will govern their children with propriety? If the father is an habitual gambler, drunkard and desperado, will not the son be so too?

The truth is, there is no attention paid to the moral, mental or physical discipline of youth in this country. They are left to their own will and inclination, to grow up, like the plants and weeds in a neglected garden, without culture or training. Surrounded as they are with so many examples of depravity, what sort of men and women are they likely to be? It is probable that the world has never reared such a horde of accomplished scamps and vagabonds, male and female, as will soon emerge from the adolescent population of the Eureka State. The signs of the times warrant this conclusion. How can it be otherwise when they are familiar with every vice, and strangers to every virtue? It matters not how strict or careful the parents themselves may be, it is impossible for them to shield their children from the baneful influences of the neighborhood; and a man might as well think of raising a healthy and stalwart family in the midst of a malarious swamp, as to think of rearing decent sons and daughters in California. The boys persuade themselves that they are men before they are half matured; and their superiors are either too little concerned about it, or too deeply engrossed in business to teach them better. As a consequence of this precocious manliness, they give themselves up to all the pernicious habits and indulgences of older reprobates.

A few words now in regard to this town of Sonora. It is built upon the slope of a long hill, and contains about four thousand inhabitants. Only one street traverses it. Unlike most other towns, its length is very much disproportioned to its breadth. As well as I remember, it is something over a mile long, and only about one hundred yards wide; so that the single street which passes through it affords an ample avenue for the intercourse and business operations of the people. The houses, or, more properly speaking, the shanties, are built close together, and open on the street, in city style. Indeed, it is here called a city, and is governed by a mayor and common council. In fact, every collection of houses in this country, every hamlet, every village, every town, is called a city. No matter if there be only half a dozen houses in a place, it is termed a city, always taking the name of the locality upon which it is built, as Collusi city, Stanislaus city, Marin city. I have visited two or three of these California "cities" that contained but a couple of frail tenements each, and four or five old bachelor inhabitants.

Before it was ascertained which were the natural or most suitable and convenient parts of the State for city sites and trading posts, there was a wonderful deal of finesse practiced by a set of land-speculators. Scattering themselves over the country, they laid claim to certain eligible plats, which, according to their stories, Nature had formed expressly for capitals and queen cities. Large maps, margined with laudatory remarks, setting forth the peerless advantages of this place and that, were committed to oily-tongued agents for general circulation. The people were informed that such a place was destined to become a metropolis, that all the surrounding mountains, hills, valleys and plains were bound to become tributary to it, that the great system and machinery of the world could not move on harmoniously without it, and that those who secured the first choice of lots would at once be in possession of a lordly fortune. This, as a matter of course, was all sheer humbug; nevertheless, in California, where humbug mingles with every transaction of life, and where people are ever ready to lay hold of any scheme that promises money, it had the desired effect.

Many persons had confidence in these projects, and made investments in them. Besides several individual cases of which I might speak, I am acquainted with a company of men who laid out more than one hundred and fifty thousand dollars in this questionable species of property;—to-day their investment is not worth two cents on the dollar. It was perfectly amusing sometimes to witness the working of these bastard enterprises. The authors and agents of the plan, having their topographic charts and every thing in readiness, would bustle about among the people, pointing out and explaining the favorable and commanding situation of the place, assuring them that the attention of the whole country was now directed to it, and giving the most exaggerated accounts of the demand for lots. In this way they would soon get up a great excitement, (it requires but a small matter to excite the people in California.) In a few instances, as many as seventy or eighty persons have been known to purchase interests in one of these bubble cities, and, laying aside all other business, flock to it without delay. Three weeks afterwards, there would probably be only one or two men on the ground, and no marks or vestiges of a city, except, perhaps, a few deserted cloth tents. It must be admitted that the projectors of these ephemeral cities made money at the expense of their victims.

The Americans were the principal operators in these speculative movements; but I know several Germans, who, though proverbially cautious in the matter of dollars and cents, were likewise drawn into them. In one particular case, two worthy representatives of the *Faderland* bought four lots, each forty-five by one hundred and thirty-seven feet, for thirteen thousand dollars, which they afterwards offered to me at ninety-five per cent. discount! I would not have taken the whole or any part of the plot at the rate of six dollars an acre.

I have alluded, parenthetically, to the excitability of the Californians. This is a remarkable trait in their character. The least thing of unusual occurrence fires their fancy and sets them in motion. If a terrier catches a rat, or if a big turnip is brought to market, the people cluster together and scramble for a sight with as much eagerness and impetuosity as a party of children would scramble after a handful of sweetmeats. If, in these hasty gatherings, one man happens to tread on the toes of another, it only requires one minute for the injured party to shoot the offender, two minutes for some body else to stab the shooter, and three minutes for the whole crowd to hang the stabber.

While in and about Sonora, we may have an opportunity of inspecting all the various systems of mining that are carried on in California. The whole earth, for some distance around, is literally turned upside down, or inside out. On the left, they are using the common single-hand rocker; on the right, sluicing; and in another place, sinking deep shafts. We shall here find a great many Mexican miners, who make deep pits and excavations in the hills, and who are generally very successful in their operations. These delving countrymen of Santa Anna seem to have a peculiar tact for discovering the veins of gold. But they do not confine themselves much to surface diggings. They have a greater propensity for holes. Sometimes they will go forty or fifty feet into the earth without finding an atom of the precious metal; but it is very seldom that they mistake their ground; they keep going, either in a perpendicular, horizontal or meandering direction, until they strike the ore. Except in working quartz veins, machinery has been but little employed, as yet, in developing the mineral resources of the State; but I am inclined to the opinion that it might be advantageously applied in gathering the gold in whatever form it may exist.

A part of the preceding chapter was devoted to observations upon the habits of life and personal appearance of the miner; but I neglected to mention his peculiar characteristic or appendage: this is the long hair upon his head and face. He neither shaves nor shears; he has no use for either razors or scissors. The tonsorial art is, in his estimation, a most reprehensible and unmanly innovation. Looking upon it as one of the fashionable foibles of society, he disavows all connection with it. He believes that Nature is not apt to make mistakes, that all things were created about right, that hair was placed upon man's head and face to harmonize with the other organs of his body, that it has its distinct and peculiar offices to perform, and that if it is cut, the whole animal economy will be more or less enervated. Such is something of the faith of the miner upon this interesting subject, which has of late been such a theme of discussion among the mustachioed and non-mustachioed world.

I confess myself, in fact, a convert to his notions. To say that the whiskers or the hair should never be trimmed, would be as much as to say that the finger-nails should never be pared; while to say that the beard or the hair should be cut close to the skin, would be the same as saying that the finger-nails should be pulled out by the roots. If we shave the chin and the cheeks, why not the head, the hands and the arms? How comes it that hair is less tolerable on the side of the face than on the back of the hand? The Chinaman shaves his head all over, except a small spot on the crown, about twice the size of a dollar, and we laugh at him for doing so; but may it not be questioned which is the greater object of derision, a bald head or a beardless face? We are also in the habit of ridiculing young ladies because they lace or compress their waists, but would it not be equally becoming in them to sneer at us for disfiguring our faces? What would we think of the belles, if they were to get in the habit of wearing false whiskers? Would we not characterize the introduction of such a fashion as a silly and whimsical innovation? But is it any more ridiculous or censurable in a woman to make her face masculine, than it is in a man to make his feminine?

That the beard is a protection against sore throats, coughs, colds, asthma, and other ailments, every California miner will be willing to testify. It is said that the English colliers, who have long suffered from hemorrhage of the lungs, have evaded the disease altogether by discontinuing the use of the razor. Yet the newspapers inform us that the clerks in the Bank of England are not allowed to wear mustachios, under penalty of dismission.

As I have heretofore remarked, mining in California is one of the most precarious of all occupations. Yet it is the country's only source of wealth, and if the laborer fails in it, he cannot betake himself to other pursuits. If he cannot make money by digging, shoveling and rocking, he cannot make it at all. Now and then, it is true, the miner meets with unanticipated good luck; but when such a thing occurs it is blazoned from Dan to Beersheba, whereas no mention is ever made of the thousands of unfortunate, poverty-stricken dupes, who, though equally industrious and deserving, scarcely defray their expenses.

I may refer to the case of an old man, who, for some time, was engaged in mining operations at this place, and with whom I became acquainted soon after my arrival here. Sixty years had left their traces upon his face, and his snowy beard and silver locks increased his venerable air. For a man of his age, he was remarkably vigorous; and as he was somewhat above the usual height, and well proportioned, with a kind heart that beamed through his intelligent features, he must have been, in his younger days, a noble specimen of a man. Even at the time of which we speak, he was a fine looking man, old in years but young in spirit, whole-souled, free from every species of hypocrisy, plain-spoken, full of courage and resolution, yet sincere and guileless as a child. Though I never saw him have on a clean shirt, though his whole garb was besmeared with mud and soiled with perspiration; though his hoary locks hung about his breast and shoulders in unrestrained length and unlimited profusion; and though he was nothing now but a poor, penniless old miner—yet, convinced that he had those excellent qualities within, which constitute the great and good man, I should have felt proud to call him father.

We will let this venerable sexagenarian tell his own story. I indite his own words, as nearly as I recollect them. Said he, during conversation one evening, after we had both quit work, "Some men would esteem themselves wealthy, if they were worth as much money as I was deprived of by bad legislation in Congress, a while previous to my departure for this country. Soon after the enactment of the tariff law of 1842, one of my neighbors and myself invested eighty thousand dollars in the manufacture of iron, in the State of Pennsylvania. Our business succeeded beyond our expectations; and in order to supply the increasing demands for our products, we found it necessary to employ additional force and capital, build new forges, and otherwise enlarge the sphere of our operations. Every examination of our affairs developed new evidences of prosperity, and our hearts glowed with gratitude to those sterling patriots and sagacious statesmen, Clay, Webster and others, through whose eloquent influence we were then harvesting the fruits of a protective tariff. But this thriving state of things was not of long continuance. In 1846 the tariff act of '42 was repealed; and that repeal was the death-blow to our manufacturing interests. The duty on iron was reduced so low that it was impossible for us to compete with the importations from Europe. We became embarrassed, made an assignment, and finally, by sacrificing every thing we had in the shape of property, extricated ourselves from all liabilities. After this stroke of misfortune, having a wife and three daughters, who were partly dependent upon me for support, I concluded to come to California, believing, from the flattering accounts which I had seen published, that money was more easily accumulated here than in the Atlantic States. It is now almost two years since I arrived in San Francisco. Going to the northern mines first, I worked there something over twelve months; but finding it a difficult matter to pay expenses, I came south, and settled at this place. I fear I have not bettered my condition. During the last seven or eight months I have labored faithfully upon this bar, but have not been in possession of as much as twenty-five dollars clear money at any one time. I confess I am utterly disappointed in California. It has been grossly, shamefully misrepresented. I have tried it to my satisfaction. Now I would be glad to return to my home in Pennsylvania, but I have no means to convey me. And there is my poor family, my beloved wife and daughters—what will become of them? May heaven provide for them, for I am unable."

As the good old man uttered these last words, the tears trickled down his cheeks, and he could say no more. Had it not been that I disdained to moisten California soil with such precious drops, I believe my eyes would have rained too; for the clouds began to gather about them, and I had to use no little precaution to keep them dry. It was certainly no sign of a white-livered man, to shed tears in a case of this kind; on the contrary, it was, at least in my opinion, a mark of goodness; and my estimation of the old gentleman was heightened, on account of the tender regard he manifested towards his family. He had lately received a most soothing and affectionate letter from one of his daughters, urging him by all means to return home on the first opportunity, and promising to exert herself to the utmost to make him happy. Handing the letter to me, he remarked that I might read it if I felt so disposed. A peculiar thrill electrified my whole system as I laid hold of the delicately penned missive. I was but little acquainted with that kind of literature, yet there was a charm about it, and I devoured its contents with avidity. It was a rare souvenir—beautifully written, well worded, and faultless in orthography.

CHAPTER XIV.

VOYAGE TO CALIFORNIA VIA CAPE HORN.

Among our readers there may be some who are contemplating a trip to California, and may be hesitating between the two routes commonly traveled. For their sakes, I have violated the chronological order of my adventures, that I might introduce a description of the outward and return trip, in immediate juxtaposition for the greater convenience of comparison.

From the pier of Wall street, New York, on Friday, January 31st, seven passengers, myself amongst the number, embarked for San Francisco, on board the clipper ship Stag-Hound, under command of Capt. Josiah Richardson. The wind blowing from the north-east afforded us a favorable opportunity for standing out from land; of this, however, we did not avail ourselves until about 4 o'clock in the afternoon; for, although our vessel was towed out early in the morning, and every thing seemed to be in readiness for our final departure, yet, through some unavoidable delay, we were obliged to cast anchor off Staten Island, where it became necessary for us to remain until the time above mentioned. We then weighed anchor, set sail, and in a few minutes our noble ship was gliding over the blue waves with swan-like grace.

It was truly a magnificent sight, as we headed off so smoothly and so majestically from the shore, and made our way out farther and farther upon the dark blue deep; we spent the greater part of the evening promenading the quarter-deck, and admiring the enchanting scene. But our reverie and conversation were not altogether undisturbed by melancholy thought. We had just started upon a long, uncertain and monotonous voyage. Old associations had been broken up. We had bid adieu to our native homes, our nearest relations and dearest friends, probably for three or four years—possibly for ever. All before us then was an unknown world—an untrodden path, and phantom-faces of doubt and fear would loom up from the obscurity of the future.

The next morning I began to feel symptoms of that most intolerable of all sensations, sea-sickness. Of this malady I had some little experience once before, while on my way from Philadelphia to New York via Cape May; but I never entertained the least idea that it was half so depressing as I now found it. For three weeks and more I could scarcely eat a mouthful. It really seemed to me at times that eating was the most abominable occupation men could engage in; and when I looked upon dishes of which I had often freely partaken before coming on board the vessel, I either found it difficult to reconcile myself to the opinion that I was not dreaming, or came well nigh detesting myself for having ever been addicted to so gross a habit.

The monotony of our daily life was without variety for the next four or five days. The wind had been somewhat favorable, and we were making good progress until the evening of the fifth day, when suddenly the wind changed and we shortly after found ourselves in the midst of as nice a hurricane as ever sunk a ship or leveled a forest. The wind howled and shrieked in such a manner that I could compare it with nothing earthly; the sea, too, had assumed, by this time, a most formidable appearance; the rain was falling in perfect torrents—the lightning flashed incessantly, and such deafening thunder-peals mortal man never heard before. It appeared as if the elements, for the last five days or so, had been nursing their wrath for this particular occasion, and were determined that we, poor devils of passengers, should be made thoroughly acquainted with the comforts of a crowded ship in a tornado at sea.

The poor affrighted passengers (myself among the rest) despaired of the ship long before the severest part of the tempest was felt, and prayers and promises were offered up without stint for our salvation, by many that never prayed before and I suppose have never done so since. When morning dawned it seemed as if the fury of the storm increased—sea and sky were apparently as one; every thing, and every body appeared helpless, hopeless, panic-stricken. Most of our canvas had been taken in or closely furled, yet the ship dashed along with the speed of a race-horse. Things that were not well secured rolled about in the greatest disorder and confusion. The heavy seas which she had already shipped, and the still heavier ones she was then shipping, increased, if possible, the consternation inspired by the awful scene. In fact, things began to wear such a threatening aspect, that a speedy change of some sort was looked forward to with the greatest anxiety, not only by the passengers, but by the captain and crew, when, to complete our terrors, topgallant-masts, royals, and main-top-mast, with their appendages, came down with a crash that was heard above the howling of the storm. By this time the day had been spent, and night considerably advanced, — with fear and trembling we retired to our state-rooms, doubting whether we should ever be permitted to see the light of another day. For myself, I suppose I was quite as indifferent about the matter as any one else; for, when a person gets to be as much under the influence of nausea as I was at the time, any change is desirable, even though it carry him to the bottom of the deep. The night passed, and we found that the storm was beginning to abate, so that, in about forty-eight hours thereafter, its violence had entirely ceased, and fine weather attended us across the equator.

The loss of our masts, in this severe gale, at once threw a damper on our high hopes of a quick passage; but, fortunately for us, we had extra masts on board; and, through the indefatigable exertions and perseverance of our vigilant captain, we succeeded in getting all the wreck cleared away and jury-masts rigged. The shattered timbers and torn sails opened an unusually large field of labor for our carpenter and sail-maker. We kept on our course, which had been very nearly south-east ever since we started, until we passed the Cape Verde Islands, about four degrees to the west, when we steered due south, and crossed the equator between twenty-nine and thirty degrees west longitude.

The next interesting event that happened to us occurred off the coast of Brazil, in latitude 22° 25′—longitude 38° 29′, Sunday, March 2d. It was about six o'clock in the morning, and I had just left my state-room and gone on deck to take a bath, when a sailor by my side, pointing over the starboard bow, cried out, "Boat ahoy! boat ahoy! with men in it." In an instant, as if by electricity, the news was conveyed to every ear on board, and, at the same time, the starboard rail was lined fore and aft with anxious sailors and half-dressed passengers. As we drew near them, (they had been rowing towards us all the while as hard as they could pull,) they commenced waving their hands and handkerchiefs, beckoning to us and calling out in an unintelligible language, as if imploring us to receive them on board. At the time, the sea was running moderately high, and we were gliding along at the rate of five or six knots per hour, so that in a few minutes we had them directly astern of us; but we were not so destitute of humanity as to pass them by and leave them to certain death. Our sympathies were quickly and enthusiastically aroused in their behalf, and as soon as our captain could get his ship under proper command, he hove her to and waited for them to row along side. Pretty soon they came close under the lee of our vessel, and their weather-beaten features and nautical garb at once gave evidence that they were not unacquainted with the life of sea-faring men.

A rope was thrown to them and they were all able to pull themselves on board by it, except one, whom we afterwards ascertained to be their captain,—he, poor fellow, was so much exhausted that he could not help himself, and we were obliged to hoist him in. Their story was the next thing to be learned; for, as yet, not a word they said had been understood. This difficulty was removed, however, as soon as we got our men collected; for, among our polyglot assemblage of men, representing nearly forty different nations, we quickly found an interpreter in the person of an old Swede, whose translation of their story was, in substance, as follows:—They were Swedes and belonged to the Russian brig Sylphide, which had been to Rio and taken in a cargo of eighteen hundred and twenty-five bags of coffee, with which they had set sail for Helsingfors, Finland,—when five days out from Rio, a severe storm, or rather squall, came upon them, and so completely and suddenly wrecked their vessel, that they had barely time to escape in one of the little boats with their lives—not even having an opportunity to procure so much as a bottle of water or a mouthful of food. So precipitate and unexpected was the calamity which thus overtook them, that they had to quit their brig without any preparation whatever, and abandon their carpenter, who happened to be in his berth sick at the time, to a watery grave.

They had been out three days and nights in this condition, with nothing to eat or drink, save the legs of their captain's boots, which they said they had been chewing to sustain life. Exposed as they were to the burning rays of a tropical sun, without any thing to eat or drink, it is not reasonable to suppose that they would have lived more than three days longer at farthest, if we had not picked them up, or if they had not been otherwise providentially relieved. We received the captain in our own cabin, and at our own table, and entertained him as hospitably and agreeably in every way as it was possible for us to do. His men went before the mast, and proved a very acceptable addition to our crew, especially in doubling Cape Horn, for they could endure the cold much better than our own seamen. That day, in commendation of the act we had performed in the morning, our captain,—who, by the by, was a very exemplary and devout scion of an orthodox Yankee house,—read, during divine service, the parable of the Good Samaritan.

About three o'clock in the afternoon of the same day, a little circumstance came under my observation, which, though it may seem quite a trivial affair in the eyes of many, may nevertheless serve to illustrate in some degree the barbarity of man and his utter indifference in regard to the lives of inferior animals. The subject of the incident was a small land bird, very much resembling our hedge sparrow, which was discovered resting upon one of the larboard main braces. A gust or blast of wind had probably driven it out to sea, and it could not find its way back to the shore. It was so weak that it could scarcely fly, and looked as if it was almost dead. On seeing it, I ran below and got a few crumbs of bread and strewed them along over the life-boat nearest to it. But just at that moment, the Swedish captain, who had now begun to resuscitate, came up on deck; and spying the distressed little wanderer, he walked up as boldly and deliberately to the rope upon which it was sitting, as if it had been some noxious intruder, and shook it violently. Thus frightened, the bird flew off some distance from the ship, but soon returned and alighted in the very same place; again the captain shook the rope as he had done at first, and again the bird did just as it had done before. This same thing was repeated for the third time, when the wearied little creature, apparently disgusted with the brutality of the man, who but a few hours before was himself in a forlorn and helpless condition, dropped down upon the water, and was seen no more.

Keeping along down the South American coast, we passed between Patagonia and the Falkland Islands; and on the morning of the 21st of March were within twenty miles of Staten Land. This was the first land we had seen since leaving home, and we feasted our eyes upon it, until our ship bore us so far distant that it had dwindled down to a mere speck. When we were near enough to Staten Land, I could see with the aid of the captain's spy-glass nothing but rugged and sterile mountains, the highest peaks of which were covered with snow, and presented quite a picturesque appearance. No vegetation nor living thing of any kind could be discerned. But a young Bostonian, whom we afterwards saw in Valparaiso, told us he passed so near the shore of some of the land lying at the southern extremity of Patagonia, that he could see the natives, who, he said, were a gigantic people, about eight feet high! He also said they ran along on the shore abreast of his vessel, whooping and yelling at him like a set of ferocious savages. On Sunday following we saw Cape Horn, the most notorious of all places upon the high seas for rough weather and contrary winds.

Up to this time we had been congratulating ourselves upon the auspicious season in which we had happened to reach the Cape, and upon the quick run we were going to make around it. Delightful weather and favorable winds had cheered us since leaving the latitude of the La Plata river, and we were in high hopes that we had just hit upon the right time to sail safely round the dangerous Cape in one or two days, instead of being kept there six or eight weeks, as is sometimes the case. But we were doomed to sad disappointment. Towards night that terror of all navigators, a downright Cape Horn tempest, assailed us, and for seven successive days and nights kept us almost completely submerged. During the whole of this time, the wind, which was so intolerably cold and piercing that it seemed to be charged with isicles, blew right in our teeth, and brought hail, sleet, rain or snow with it every hour. Owing to this hard and continued blowing of the wind, the size and power of the waves became perfectly appalling; indeed they ran so heavy and so high that each one looked like a little ocean of itself, and frequently they would strike the ship with such tremendous force that she quivered and groaned as if she were going to pieces; in fact, I often expected to see her shivered into fragments, and could hardly believe otherwise than that we were all destined to become food for the fierce monsters of the deep. We succeeded, however, in getting fairly around the Cape, much to the gratification of all, and especially to the relief of our worn-out seamen, who had been up working with all their might, day and night, for a whole week.

While in the neighborhood of the Cape, we saw great numbers of the albatross, gull, petrel, and other birds; by means of a fish-hook tied to the end of a long line, and baited with a piece of fat bacon, which we let out some eight or ten rods from the stern of the vessel, we caught several of a species which the sailors called the

Cape Hen. On measuring one of them from the tip of its right wing to the tip of its left, I found it to be seven feet across. The albatross is about twice as large as the Cape Hen. Here, too, while in this latitude, we had our fairest views of the great Southern Cross and the Magellan Clouds, constellations of as much notoriety in the southern hemisphere, as the Pleiades and Belt of Orion are in the northern.

It seems that the Atlantic and Pacific oceans are ever at war with each other off Cape Horn, where their waters are continually coming into mad collision, as if no friendship existed between them. But we will now bid adieu to this aquatic battle field, this bleak, dreary region of storms and hurricanes, and look forward to a more congenial clime.

Finding our water was now beginning to give out, and that we should have to procure a fresh supply before we could reach San Francisco, we bent our course towards Valparaiso, upon the coast of Chili, south of the city and harbor to which we were then bound; and as we passed along up the shore, we had a most magnificent view, not only of its own long range of barren hills, but also of the lofty and towering heights of the Andes at the distance of one hundred and forty-five miles in the interior. To add to the grandeur of this spectacle on land, another now presented itself on the ocean around us, in the form of great whales—the first we had seen. We saw many of these huge creatures that day and the next; one of them came within two or three rods of the stern of the ship, and spouted the water with a noise something like that of a high pressure Mississippi steamboat.

We had scarcely dropped our anchor in the harbor of Valparaiso before we were surrounded with little boats filled with natives and foreigners, who had come out, as they said, to talk with us and to see our ship. From these men we learned that four days previously a severe earthquake had been felt, and that all the houses in the city had been more or less injured—a part of the city completely destroyed, and some few persons killed. It was also reported by some of them, that it had laid a great portion of Santiago, the capital, in ruins; but, as yet, no definite news had been received from any of the inland cities or towns; and it was not positively ascertained what amount of damage had been sustained in any place, save only here. Late that evening, about half an hour before sundown, we passengers made our entrance into the city; but it was then too late in the day to see or learn any thing of interest, so we returned directly to our own quarters aboard the ship, and waited in suspense for the coming morn.

Immediately after an early breakfast, Wednesday morning, we put off in a small boat for the shore, and were not a little surprised on arriving there to find every thing so new and so different from what we had supposed. Crowds of the natives, dressed in their peculiar costume, were collected upon the wharves, and were making a great hubbub with their clamorous tongues and noisy actions. They appeared to be an inoffensive, simple-hearted sort of people; but they were inexcusably ignorant, and abominably filthy.

Scarcely had we been in the city half an hour that morning, when I stepped into a barber-shop to have the superfluous hair removed from my head and face. While in the very act of shaving me, the barber very suddenly sprang aghast from me towards the door; and the first thing I knew, the whole earth, houses and every thing around me, were quivering in the most terrific manner; but, fortunately for the timid, helpless creatures, the vacillation continued but a few seconds, and no very serious consequences resulted from it. Just at the moment the rumbling and quaking commenced, I could not for my life think what it was; but the barber seemed to understand it immediately, for he had been the unwilling spectator of a much more destructive earthquake only five days before; and consequently, he knew well enough what the matter was. On retiring from the shop, just as I entered the street, a similar shock was experienced, and instantaneously the whole population rushed headlong out of their houses into the thoroughfares, apparently in the greatest distress, and frightened half out of their wits. I observed several of the women particularly, who, upon running into the streets, immediately placed themselves in an attitude of prayer, by falling upon their knees, crossing their hands upon their breasts, and casting their eyes towards heaven. There was something really beautiful and touching in the unfeigned humility with which these awe-struck mortals resigned themselves to the will of Him who alone is able to convulse worlds, or command tranquillity throughout the universe.

Both of these tremors were slight, and neither did much mischief. But the one that occurred four days previous to our arrival came very near laying the whole city in ruins. The custom house, churches, stores, and nearly all the principal buildings were cracked so badly that many of them were considered dangerous. The people were engaged in pulling down some entirely, and repairing others as best they could. The ground was terribly rent in many places; and while on a stroll beyond the limits of the city, I saw one crevasse which was about five inches in width, and so long and so deep that I could find neither end nor bottom to it. We remained in Valparaiso till the afternoon of Saturday, but did not feel any other shock. For myself, I was satisfied with what I saw then, and having been since shaken by them two or three times during my sojourn in California, I hope I shall never feel another.

As for the city itself, we saw nothing that was really beautiful about it. The majority of the residences were built of mud and straw, and covered with tiles; and were, I think, upon the whole, rather inferior to the negro huts upon a southern plantation. The immense sterile hills all round, about, and through the city, presented quite a dreary and desolate appearance, and prevented us from seeing more than half the number of its buildings at the same time. One of the merchants, a New Orleans man, informed me that the population was estimated at from 60,000 to 65,000. Speaking of this merchant reminds me of a remarkable instance of stupidity which came under my observation one morning while visiting his store. He had just received fifty barrels of pork, which the drayman had left before his door, and which he wished to have stowed in his cellar. His regular porter being sick, he hired two doltish countrymen to perform the job. It was stipulated that they should receive a certain sum of money for removing the pork from the street into the cellar; and the bargain being fairly understood on both sides, they began to fulfil their part of the contract, by *lifting* the barrels instead of rolling them. We allowed them to pursue this tòilsome system of labor until they had finished about one fifth of their task, when we interposed and explained to them the easier method of accomplishing it. It is a fact, according to their own confession, that they had not sense enough to avail themselves of the rotundity of the barrels.

Valparaiso surpasses San Francisco in the abruptness of its surface and the barrenness of its soil. There is no plant within sight of the town, except here and there in the little vales and hollows. The inhabitants have to bring all their supplies from beyond the coast range, a distance of nine or ten miles; and as the hills are so large and so steep that they cannot be traversed with vehicles, every thing must be transported upon the backs of mules. The interior of Chili is represented to be a very beautiful and productive country; and, to use the language of her historian, "all the fruits of the earth grow there in the greatest abundance." Towards noon that day, we chartered some donkeys and rode out about two miles, to a garden called the Vale of Paradise, in the upper part of the city. This was one of the most charming spots I ever beheld, and, with the exception of two or three other little places like it, the only level and fertile piece of ground we saw during the whole time we were there. Here, on the 9th of

April, we got apples, pears, peaches, pomegranates, pine apples, quinces, oranges, lemons, figs, bananas, mangoes and melons, to our hearts' content.

On Thursday, having wandered from my comrades, I began to perambulate the streets alone, determined to see and learn as much of the city as practicable. At last I found I had wandered very nearly to its northern outskirts, when I came to a little winding path, which I followed up till it led me to the opened gate of a beautiful, palisaded inclosure. Upon looking in I observed a long, clean, level walk in the midst of the most delectable garden I ever saw. All the way overhead, from one end of the walk to the other, there were large, luscious clusters of grapes, hanging down in the richest profusion; while on either side there seemed to be an actual rivalry in growth and luxuriance between the various fruits and vegetables. About half way up the walk, in a well shaded place, two middle-aged men, dressed in long robes, and with books in their hands, were sitting on a bench, reading. Still I continued to stand at the gate, admiring the fascinating scenery before me, being seen by nobody, and seeing no one myself, except the two gownsmen, whose attention seemed to be wholly absorbed by their books. To go in I feared would not only be an interruption to the quietude and serenity which pervaded those elysian grounds, but also an intrusion upon the privacy of gentlemen whom I had no right to disturb. However, hoping to frame a reasonable excuse by offering to purchase some fruit, I stepped in, and slowly approaching the literary group, inquired, "Do you speak English?" Scarcely had the words fallen from my tongue, when the one who sat farthest from me arose, and having replied in the affirmative, extended his hand towards me in a very cordial manner, and then asked me a long question in Latin, not a word of which I understood except the termination, which was "St. Patrick?" Manifesting by my looks, as well as I could, my ignorance of his ecclesiastical salutation, interrogation, or whatever it was, he immediately dropped his classical lore, and conversed with me freely in English—both of us, in the meantime, promenading up and down the lovely arbor. From him I learned that the adjoining buildings were occupied as a Roman Catholic college, and that this garden was exclusively for the use and benefit of the priests, of whom he was one, as well as a professor in the institution. He informed me that it was the largest and most popular college in Chili, and that they had students from nearly all the republics and provinces of the continent. He himself was a native of Belgium, but had emigrated to South America as a missionary some fifteen years prior to the time I saw him. The book he then held in his hand was a Spanish history of the United States; and as he asked me a great many questions concerning our country, I inferred that he felt a good deal of interest in it. Upon the whole, he appeared to be a very kind-hearted and well-disposed man. Just before leaving, he presented me with a mammoth bunch of delicious grapes, and at parting, gave my hand a courteous and sincere shake.

At this place we parted with the wrecked crew we had picked up five weeks before, leaving them in the hands of the Russian consul. But before bidding a final adieu to the captain, we purchased a gold ring and inclosed it in a sympathizing epistle to his wife, condoling with her in her husband's misfortunes. When we committed the letter and little keepsake to his charge, he seemed to be very much affected, and acknowledged himself under a thousand obligations to us.

Little occurred on our passage from Valparaiso to San Francisco worthy of note, except the myriads of fish of various kinds which we saw between the tropics, the sublime sunrises and sunsets, the enchanting moonlight evenings, and the phosphorescent phenomena of the ocean at night. The Pacific far surpasses the Atlantic in beauty and diversity of ocean scenery. Its gentle gales and placid waves inexpressibly charm the heart of the sailor. Almost every species of fish, from the tiny pilchard to the monstrous whale may be found in its waters; while countless numbers of aquatic birds, from the diminutive petrel to the ponderous albatross, swim lazily upon its bosom.

Six days after leaving Valparaiso we passed within a short distance of the St. Felix Islands, which rise alone out of the world of water. We could see nothing that had life in it about them, nor any thing that was inviting or pleasing to the eye. On the morning of the 5th May, we again crossed the equator, in longitude 114°.

This voyage afforded us an excellent opportunity for reading; but it may well be supposed that, in traveling seventeen thousand miles upon the water, we were sometimes overcome with ennui. As a refuge from this monotony of "life on the ocean wave," we betook ourselves to games of euchre, whist, chess, backgammon and solitaire. Our ship being very large, perfectly new, beautifully and comfortably finished, and furnished with the very best accommodations, eatables and drinkables, we enjoyed ourselves remarkably well, except while sea-sick, or when dashed and beaten about by ill-bred storms and hurricanes. As there were only six passengers besides myself, we had abundance of room; and being together so long, and secluded from all other society, we became as sociable and familiar as if we had all been members of the same household. A very amiable and estimable young lady, the sister of a passenger, and the only female on board, contributed in an eminent degree to the pleasure of the trip.

We arrived in San Francisco on the 25th of May, having made the passage in one hundred and thirteen days from New York. This was a very quick run, considering the misfortunes we met with off the Bermudas. If we had not been dismasted, we would probably have reached our destination twelve or fifteen days earlier. The Flying Cloud, clipper-modeled, and built almost exactly like the Stag Hound, ran from New York to San Francisco in eighty-nine days, which is the shortest voyage that has yet been made by a sailing vessel between the two ports. Many of the old-fashioned ships crawl along for seven or eight months; and I know one blunt, tub-like carac which consumed three hundred and seventy days in the passage.

CHAPTER XV.

VOYAGE FROM CALIFORNIA VIA NICARAGUA.

About six hundred homeward-bound passengers, myself included, left San Francisco on the 16th of March, in the splendid steamship Cortes, under command of Captain Cropper. It being our intention to reach the Caribbean sea by the Nicaragua route, we bent our course towards San Juan del Sur. Wind and wave both favored our movements, and we made rapid progress. Stray thoughts occupied my mind as my eyes rested for the last time upon the barren hills of California. There I had witnessed many strange sights and incidents. Should I ever see them again? Was it probable that I would stop to renew my acquaintance with them while on my way to Japan and China in 1875, by the great Atlantic and Pacific railway? My mind, however, was occupied but a little while in the consideration of these matters. There was before me a country which engendered a brighter train of thoughts than that which I was leaving behind. I began to think of greeting the good old folks at home; of joining long-parted hands, and of roaming over the glades and glens which first supported my tottering steps.

Our gallant ship continued to glide bravely on towards the place of her destination. Neither accident nor rough weather happened to us, and we should have enjoyed ourselves finely if there had not been so many persons on board. The crowd was too large for a pleasure party at sea. There were too many mouths to feed, too many berths to adjust, and too many complaints to be heard. Somebody was always in the way of somebody else. We were too much pent up. There was an abundance of room all around us, above and below us; but it was not adapted to our purposes. The Cortez was our only foothold; and it was necessary that we should cling to her as the only means of reaching terra firma.

But I imagine those of us who had state-rooms on the cabin-deck would not have felt any disposition to murmur, if we had known how much better we fared than the other passengers. Only about one hundred and fifty enjoyed this advantage; all the others were huddled together in the steerage. Is it reasonable to suppose that any considerable number of these four hundred and fifty persons would have engaged such uncomfortable and unwholesome passage, if they could have done better? No. They could scarcely have been hired to pass through the torrid zone in the steerage, if they had possessed money enough to pay for a cabin-passage. It is a well-known fact that the steamers bring a much larger number of steerage passengers from California than they take there. The majority of those that go to California take passage in the cabin; but more than two-thirds of those who return occupy the steerage. As a matter of course, there was no communication between the cabin and steerage passengers; at least those in the steerage were not allowed to come abaft the ship; but I do not think our privileges were circumscribed in this respect, for I went forward of the bulkhead several times, as did many others who belonged in the cabin, and the officers said nothing to us.

There was quite a medley of characters in the cabin. Bishop Soule, of the Methodist Episcopal Church, South, may be placed at the head. He is a stout, fine-looking old gentleman, about seventy years of age; and I sincerely believe he was the best man aboard the vessel. He had been stirring up the sinners in California for some time, and was now returning to his home in Georgia. Next came the Rev. Dr. Boring and three or four other clergymen, one of whom had formerly been a missionary in Brazil. The Secretary of Utah Territory, a downright jolly fellow, dressed in a suit of buckskin, and who, while on the Isthmus, manifested a most ardent passion for parrots, was also on board. Besides these, there were eight colonels, seven majors, five captains, three professors, six doctors, ten quacks, five lawyers, eight pettifoggers, a score of blacklegs, six or eight ladies, a dozen other adult females, and fifteen or twenty children. We also had the company of a Polish patriot, who was on his way to the East to join the Turkish army.

On the seventh or eighth day after our departure from San Francisco, one of the passengers, while taking spy-glass observations, espied a motionless object at a great distance on the water—the sea at the time being perfectly calm and smooth. The spy-glass passed rapidly from hand to hand, and was kept almost constantly leveled towards the object; but nobody could determine what it was. One man thought it a ship in distress; another inclined to the opinion that it was abandoned altogether; while a third sighingly expressed his conviction that it was the decaying remnant of a melancholy wreck. The captain, more dispassionate, experienced, and capable of forming a correct judgment, now surveyed it carefully; but it was so far off upon the larboard quarter, that he acknowledged himself unable to give any reliable information concerning it. What then was to be done? Should we stifle our curiosity and continue on our course, or should we change and go to the mysterious object? Some favored one proposition, and some the other. Considerable betting had been going on as to the number of days we would be occupied in making the passage, and one half of those who had thus wagered their money were opposed to losing the time which it would require to make the examination. But the motion to go being seconded and sanctioned by a large majority of the passengers, the captain immediately turned the prow of the steamer.

After sailing awhile on this new track, we discovered a large flock of longipennate birds flying around the wreck to which we were then bound. This was an ominous sign. What were these sea buzzards doing about a disabled vessel, if they were not feeding on the dead bodies of seamen? But the rapid movement of the Cortez assured us that our curiosity should soon be allayed. With the aid of the spy-glass we could now view the object distinctly; and on approaching still nearer, we found it was nothing but an old empty scow! and that it was frequented by the fowls of the sea merely because it afforded them a place to rest and to roost. What a sore disappointment it was, not to find the carcasses of a hundred starved sailors! A day or two after this, one of the steerage passengers died, an old sail was wrapped around him, two pieces of pig-iron were fastened to his feet, and he was cast overboard.

Early in the morning of the thirteenth day of our pilgrimage upon the water, we arrived at San Juan del Sur, a miserable, good-for-nothing little town, situated on the western coast of Nicaragua, near the eleventh parallel of north latitude. The harbor was as mean and ugly as the town, being very small, shallow and inconvenient. There were no piers nor wharves, and we had to cast anchor about one hundred and fifty yards from the shore. Large yawls were then prepared for us, and we were conveyed as near terra firma as the depth of the harbor would allow. But when the yawls struck bottom, I think we were still from twenty-five to thirty yards from the water's edge; and there were no means or facilities of reaching the shore, except by wading, or by straddling the shoulders of the half-breed, quarter-dressed natives, scores of whom, in the hope of making a few shillings, were standing waist-deep in the water all around us, and begging us to take seats on their backs, a request with which, after some deliberation, we complied.

During this novel process of debarkation, I witnessed some most ludicrous scenes. The Nicaraguans, generally speaking, are much more feeble, dwarfed, and effeminate than the people of the United States. On an average, I should think that one able-bodied Kentuckian would be equal to four or five of these hybrid denizens of the torrid zone. It will not, therefore, surprise the reader when I tell him that the small man, while carrying the large one through the water, being top-heavy, would sometimes drop his burden! Nor was this all; the ladies were yet behind, and they had to be brought ashore in the same manner!

Among our passengers were two or three oleaginous men, of Falstaff proportions; one of whom engaged a couple of the stoutest carriers around the yawl to convey him to the shore. Fixing himself upon their shoulders as well as he could, he signified to them that he was ready, and they made for land; but before they had proceeded half a dozen steps, he weighed them down, and all three fell flat on their backs in the water! This little mishap created a great deal of merriment; and several others who had just mounted and started, unable to restrain their laughter, leaned back too far to give it vent, and down they tumbled into the water likewise! It was necessary for the rider, or topmost man, to keep himself in a quiet, perpendicular position; for if he leaned backward, or forward, or sideway, he was sure to throw the carrier off his equilibrium, in which case both of them would fall down together.

The ladies had now arrived from the Cortez, and were ready to disembark. There was but one way for them to get ashore, and that has already been explained. They, too, were compelled to straddle the shoulders of the natives; and when fairly mounted, give the signal of command, and ride ahead boldly, like equestrian amazons in a circus. It may here be remarked that these men were nearly naked, there being no apparel upon them except a kind of bandage or wrapper around their loins. The manner of mounting the carrier, whose head was almost on a level with the rim of the yawl, was to place the right limb over his right shoulder, and the left over his left; and when thus conveyed to the shore, it was a very easy matter to part the limbs from his shoulders, and slide down his back. These, then, were the means and facilities which were afforded for the disembarkation of the ladies; and I have thus dwelt upon the subject for the purpose of informing my fair readers, if I have any, what they may expect upon their arrival at San Juan del Sur.

All the passengers and baggage were now landed, and after a deal of vexation in securing checks and transit tickets, we set forward across the country in the direction of Virgin Bay, a shabby village, situated about fifteen miles distant, on Lake Nicaragua. We traveled this part of the way on donkeys. The roads were in pretty fair condition, and a few of the ladies, being well skilled in horsemanship, rode sideways, but the majority of them having but little knowledge of equestrian exercises, rode like men. This was my first entrance into the dismal glories of a tropical forest. The trees pressed against each other for room, and were clothed with the heaviest and most luxuriant foliage I ever beheld, presenting every tint and shade of green. Coppice and parasites filled up the interstices between them. Myriads of gay-plumaged birds warbled upon their branches. Ten thousand times ten thousand insects chirped beneath their limbs. Nimble monkeys ran up their trunks, and venomous reptiles slept in their shadows.

To give an idea of the weather, I will simply say that, if I intended to become a citizen of Nicaragua, I should advocate the immediate construction of three public works, namely: a government bellows, a state fan, and a great national umbrella! With the aid of these cooling machines, I should think a person might manage to keep passably comfortable; but without them, the heat is almost intolerable. In our own country, the people are apt to complain of the hot days which dawn upon them in July and August, but the caloric of the United States bears no more comparison to that of Nicaragua than a frosty morning in Carolina to a perpetual winter in Greenland.

We rode on, however, in spite of the fiery heat of the sun, and arrived at Virgin Bay in good season for dinner. There were eight or ten dirty little taverns in this despicable little town, and as it was uncertain how long we should have to wait for our baggage, which was still behind, and which was not expected before night, we placed ourselves in charge of the landlords, who were highly pleased to receive such a multitude of guests. About four o'clock in the afternoon, I went down to the lake to bathe, having been previously assured that the alligators did not frequent that side of the bay, except during the night.

The scenery here was grand beyond description. Lake Nicaragua itself may be justly termed an inland sea. It is more than one hundred miles long, and sixty miles in width. Mount Ometepe, a dormant volcano, and by far the most beautiful elevation I ever saw, rises up out of the midst of this lake, in the form of a sugar-loaf, to the height of seven thousand feet. At a rough guess, I should say it was about fifty miles in circumference at the base, or rather at the surface of the water.

A little before sunset, I returned to my hotel, and took supper. I had, however, but little appetite for culinary preparations, for I had fed myself on such a quantity of mangoes, oranges, bananas, and other tropical fruits, that I was quite surfeited. Forty or fifty hammocks were suspended in the loft of the hotel, and these were more attractive than any other part of the entertainment.

We sat up until nearly midnight, waiting for our baggage, but it did not come; and we were then informed that it would not arrive before morning. The sun arose and found us still separated from our effects. Noon came and brought the baggage with it. Thus you see we had suffered an unnecessary delay of twenty-four hours at Virgin Bay. The steamer Ometepe was now ready to receive us, and as we were all anxious to reach home, we lost no time in going aboard. From this place we sailed in a south-easterly direction until breakfast hour next morning, when we arrived at Fort San Carlos, where we entered the San Juan river, which conveys the waters of Lake Nicaragua into the Caribbean Sea. There was nothing to be seen at San Carlos, except the dilapidated fort, and it was not worth looking at. Here we had to leave the Ometepe, and embark on a smaller boat, the river being too shallow to float a vessel of deep draught.

Pursuing the current of the San Juan, we passed the unworthy little village of Castillo, and again changed boats, leaving one of sorry dimensions behind, and taking passage in a meaner one of less size, and now came the peculiar annoyance of the route. Owing to the shoals and sand banks in the river, we had to change ourselves and our baggage several times; and every change we made was from bad to worse. Those of us who had taken passage in the cabin, though we had paid more than double the price of steerage tickets, received no extra accommodation whatever. We were reduced to a level with the steerage passengers at San Juan del Sur, and no manner of distinction was made between us until we reached the opposite coast. For three days and nights we were all crowded together in utter disorder and confusion; men, women and children, white people and negroes, decent men and blackguards—all fared alike. The presence of the ladies did not seem to exercise any restraint upon the tongues of the vulgar. I am sure I had never before been in the company of a set of human beings who were capable of giving utterance to such an incessant volley of scurrilous and obscene language as I heard while crossing the Isthmus.

There was not a mouthful of victuals prepared for us on board of these miserable, rickety little steamers; nor was there any place to sleep, except on deck, among puddles of tobacco juice. Occasionally we had an opportunity of buying fruits and refreshments on the way; and this was the only method we had of procuring any thing to eat. I do not think I slept two hours out of the seventy-two which we occupied in passing the two oceans. Indeed, the Transit Company treated us very shabbily. We had paid them their price, and they had promised us better things. Sometimes, to save the steamer from running aground, we had to debark, and walk on the bank of the river. On one occasion we were compelled to travel more than two miles in this manner, before we could find water deep enough to carry us aboard the boat. As we neared the mouth of the river, we met and overtook a great many adult natives, who were in the same costume in which nature had launched them into the world. They did not seem to be conscious of any impropriety in thus exposing their persons.

Nicaragua can never fulfil its destiny until it introduces negro slavery. Nothing but slave labor can ever subdue its forests or cultivate its untimbered lands. White men may live upon its soil with an umbrella in one hand and a fan in the other; but they can never unfold or develop its resources. May we not safely conclude that negro slavery will be introduced into this country before the lapse of many years? We think so. The tendency of events fully warrants this inference.

The time may come when negro slavery will no longer be profitable in the United States; and it is also possible that the descendants of Ham may finally work their way beyond the present limits of our country. But if these fated people ever do make their exodus from the hands of their present owners, they will find themselves journeying and toiling under the control of new masters, in the fertile wildernesses and savannas nearer the equator. Louisiana and Texas may, at some future time—

far in the future—find it to their interest to adopt the white slavery system of the North; but if negro slavery ever ceases to exist in the United States, Mexico, Central America, and the countries still further South, will have to become its outlets and receptacles.

It would be no easy task to find a more feeble and ineffective population than that which now idles away a miserable existence in Nicaragua. Nature is too bountiful to the inhabitants. It supplies them with every necessary of life, and consequently there is no incentive to exertion or emulation. Countless fruits and nuts grow and ripen spontaneously, and they have nothing to do but to eat them. We did not pass a single patch of ground under cultivation; nor did I see any improvement, except the despicable little huts and shanties in which the people lived.

On the morning of the first day of April, we arrived at San Juan del Norte, alias Greytown, which has recently handed its name down to history, in connection with that of commander Hollins, by whom, in compliance with instructions from our government, it was bombarded a few months ago. We did not go on shore, but I saw enough of the place to convince me that it was never worth half the paper which has been spoiled by diplomatic notes concerning it. The Americans call it Greytown, but the original Spanish name is San Juan del Norte, which, when Anglicized, means Saint John of the North. As we have had a good deal to say respecting San Juan del Sur, it may not be amiss to state that the English of it is Saint John of the South. Just before we left the mouth of the river, we saw eight or ten full-grown alligators, basking on an islet, thirty or forty yards from us. They were all lying near each other, and did not seem to be frightened at our appearance. I was well pleased to have such a fair view of these amiable lizards, but regretted my inability to secure one for Barnum! About three hundred of our passengers waved us an adieu at Greytown, and took passage in the steamer Daniel Webster for New Orleans. The rest immediately set sail for New York, in the steamer Star of the West.

We now found ourselves happily situated where we had good order, good accommodations, and good treatment—three good things which many of us had not been accustomed to for three long years. An air of propriety and fitness pervaded the Star of the West fore and aft; and we felt as if we were emerging from a vile and debased community, and entering upon the threshold of refined society. No incident worthy of note occurred during this part of our voyage. We were in hopes the captain would stop at Kingston, Havana, or some other West India port; but he had no occasion to do so. Passing on between Cuba and Yucatan, we rounded the

Florida Reefs, and then followed the Gulf stream until we reached the latitude of Cape Hatteras, when we bore nearer the land, and ran into the harbor of New York on Sunday, April 9th, having had a passage of twenty-four days from San Francisco.

CHAPTER XVI.

MY LAST MINING ADVENTURE.

More than satisfied with the experience I had acquired in mining operations in California, I found much difficulty in deciding upon my future course. At one time I made up my mind to try what the fickle jade fortune would do for me in Australia, and even went so far as to engage a passage on board of a ship that would sail for Sydney within a week. An acquaintance and friend, to whom I imparted my intentions, earnestly persuaded me to abandon my projected voyage, and urged me to accompany him to Columbia and take an interest in a very promising mining adventure. My friend said "he felt quite sure that we could make an ounce ($16) a day each with the utmost ease, provided we were favored with sufficient rain. And as the rainy season was close at hand, he was fully satisfied that we should have as plentiful a supply of water as our mining operations would require." I had heard of these diggings frequently, and that gold was found there in great abundance, but as no stream watered these surface mines, they could only be worked during the rainy season.

As my friend's story was corroborated by my own knowledge of these things, I agreed without much hesitation to abandon my voyage to Australia, and join him in this new mining expedition—mentally resolving, however, that it should be the last of my efforts to become suddenly rich by delving for gold in the mines of California.

We left San Francisco in the latter part of the month of October, ran up the river San Joaquin to Stockton in a stern-wheel steamboat, so crowded with passengers that berths were entirely out of the question, and so we were doomed to get through the night as best we could. And *such* a night! It is my candid belief that for some unknown reason this particular night lasted as long as thirteen others combined together, and that during its continuance, I visited the infernal regions, upon the pressing invitation of a legion of fiends, all wearing Chinamen's hats and long tails; moreover, I solemnly assert that almost every winged insect and other creeping thing within a circuit of fifty leagues paid their respects to us on board that miserable little steamboat. I have a faint recollection of invoking the aid of all the saints in the calendar for relief, but they would not hear me, and so I e'en concluded to imitate great Cæsar's example at the base of Pompey's statue,—wrap my head in my mantle, and thus resign myself to inexorable fate. As to my friend, I had lost sight of him almost as soon as we entered the boat, and it was no small gratification to think that remorse had caused him to commit suicide, or some such thing. I trusted he had leaped overboard from sheer compunction of conscience for having deluded me into this scrape, and hoped by drowning himself to atone in some measure for his atrocious conduct. Poor fellow! I forgave him, and mentally resolved to get up something pathetic in the shape of an obituary notice, as thus: Departed this life, on the evening of the 25th of October, 1853, by water, one Shad Back, (real name supposed to be Shadrach Bachus,) aged 34, or thereaway. The immediate cause of his death was remorse of conscience for having decoyed an unsuspecting and virtuous youth on board of a poor miserable craft crowded with passengers, without berths, without seats, and swarming with vermin of every description, including Chinamen. It is supposed that, in a moment of despair, produced by witnessing the distress of his victim, he jumped into the river and was drowned. His numerous friends cannot but bewail his untimely end, although *some* are of the opinion that it "sarved him right." *Requiescat in pace.*

I thought I would add to this a verse or so from some suitable ditty, but could hit upon nothing that would reach the case better than a portion of Gray's Elegy, beginning: "Here rests his head upon this lap of earth," &c. Now as I was not fully convinced that "his head *did* rest upon this lap of earth," I deemed it best to change the text slightly to meet the melancholy occasion, and make it read thus:

There rests beneath the briny wave,
A youth to linen and to soap unknown;
Fair science frowned, but failed to save
This blessed youth, who then went down.

I confess my inability to state distinctly what is meant by the last line; it seemed to rhyme with "unknown," and as I never had been guilty of an attempt of this kind before, I thought it would do very well as a first effort in the line of poetry. I may as well here explain also, that as I intended to have the whole thing painted upon a good sized shingle, and that nailed upon some tree near the sea shore, I thought it would be a good idea to have the hand with an extended finger painted conspicuously on the shingle, to serve as a pointer towards the ocean; this would sufficiently explain the meaning of "*there rests,*" and "*briny wave.*"

Notwithstanding the bodily torments I underwent during that livelong night, with my head wrapped in a mantle and all the rest of my person fairly given over to the tender mercies of thousands of mosquitos, gnats, sand-flies, ants, ticks, fleas and bed-bugs, I really experienced a strong sensation of relief upon reflecting how very handsomely I had disposed of my friend's earthly affairs. At the same time I thought it quite possible that my good intentions towards his memory, coupled with the fact of my sufferings, and the pains and penalties I had undergone and was still enduring, would in a measure serve as a sort of atonement for my own sins of omission and commission, beginning far back, at a very early period of my life.

Morning dawned at last, and I was in the very act of gathering the remainder of my person into an upright position, when I heard a voice, proceeding from beneath an immense heap of Chinamen, Irishmen, and niggers, calling me by name, and entreating my assistance to get him upon his legs. I seemed to know the voice very well, but could not recall to mind the owner. Deeming it, however, the duty of a good Christian to help a distressed fellow-creature, I made my way through the crowd to the spot whence the voice issued, and there, to my intense grief and astonishment, I beheld my friend Shad upon his back, actively engaged in repelling, with hands and feet, the united assaults of a strong force, composed of three Irishmen and four Chinese fellows. I became convinced, the moment I saw his position, that if he escaped hanging for his misdemeanors in California, he would become a great general, and an ornament to the military profession. I came to this conclusion because, at the moment I saw him, he was preparing to repel the enemy in a most masterly manner. The allies were *en potence*, and had already attacked and dispersed Shad's advanced guard, making prisoners of his outlying pickets (his boots and hat) in a gallant manner. Then with a determination to conquer or die, rushed upon the main body. Here, after a most desperate struggle, during which many great deeds of daring were exhibited, the enemy were repulsed with immense loss. Much as I deprecate war in any shape, yet I could not sufficiently admire the calm and collected appearance of Shad, even when in the heat of the *melee*. One particular feat performed by one of Shad's feet, was observed by me with much astonishment, and it seemed to strike an Irishman very forcibly too, as he honored the performance by immediate prostration. The enemy had retired to a distance, and no doubt held a council of war, and from the disposition of his forces shortly after, I judged his intention was to make a demonstration upon Shad's front, and then attack him with his whole concentrated force in the rear. My conjecture proved correct. I saw in a moment that this manœuvre must prove successful, unless Shad could strengthen his flanks, or form himself into a hollow square. And here it soon became apparent how profoundly my friend had studied the art of attack and defence. A pocket edition of Vauban must have been his constant companion, or he never could have assumed such a formidable appearance as that which he now presented. Like an able general, he had divined the enemy's intentions, and to meet the emergency, had disposed his person in such a manner that he could swing himself around like a teetotum while lying upon his back, much the same as a long eighteen upon a pivot. In this position, or rather with this rotary motion, Shad was invulnerable. He presented a front in every direction, and utterly defeated the enemy's most strenuous efforts to capture him.

At this stage of the proceedings, I proposed mediating between the high contending parties, which proposal being acceded to, I forthwith decided the matter in difference, (of which I did not understand one word,) by decreeing a forfeiture of Shad's boots, the restoration of his hat, and the payment by Shad for two gallons of *red-eye* to regale the company. This last decision was received with marked respect by all but my poor friend. It was also decreed that the captured boots should belong hereafter to the most *devout* of the belligerents. Thereupon they were deposited at the feet of a boy from the sod, who, since his prostration, had been seated on deck, curved up in a manner quite curious to behold. He resembled the capital letter G as much as any thing I could think of at the time. Peace having been solemnly proclaimed, I had now an opportunity of better observing my friend Back's personal appearance. He had never been very remarkable for great personal beauty at any period of his life, and as the late battle had not left him wholly unscathed, it would have proved a great hit indeed to an artist, if he could have taken his likeness just then! When we came on board of this infernal boat, Mr. Shad Back possessed a pair of bright blue eyes, which by some uncommon process had been converted, during the night, into a pair (or rather one and a half) of dismal black ones; his nose, always flat, was now scarcely discernible at all—it had been absolutely beaten into his face; lips as thick and black as those of a Loango negro, and without a tooth in his head to save him from starvation. The fact is, my friend Shad had received as severe a mauling as one man could well stagger under; and although I pitied him truly and sincerely, yet I could not help feeling a sort of disappointment at knowing he was not drowned or dead in some way, and it *is* a great disappointment to any one, after making extensive preparations to mourn the fate of a man who he hopes will commit suicide. After he has adjusted his face and his garments to represent a decent amount of grief, and above all, after he has composed his epitaph, including therein a scrap of touching poetry, to find that he is not dead nor drowned after all, I say again, *is* a disappointment and a great shame.

But, supposing "all things are for the best," I swallowed my chagrin and a cup of (stewed mud) coffee together, resolving to write no man's epitaph until I had the sexton's certificate, or officiated in person at the crowner's or coroner's inquest.

We landed in Stockton a little before noon of the same day, and thence took passage in a lumber wagon for Columbia, in or near which place the mines were situated. Columbia is in Tuolumne county, near the base of the Sierra Nevada, and contains about 2,000 inhabitants. Its mines are said to be the richest in the State. As we had come here for the express purpose of making a fortune without let or hindrance, and with as little labor as possible, we went to work at once, digging and toiling like men determined to become millionaires within a week at the farthest. In a few days we had collected a large mass of dirt together, and only waited for rain to afford us an opportunity of testing its value. But the rain would not come. Every morning, for at least a month, Shad predicted rain in torrents, and got drunk without delay, in order, as he said, to celebrate an event of so much consequence to our future fortunes. Sure enough, the rain did come at last. It continued to fall somewhat briskly for about an hour, then it ceased for an hour or so. Again it fell for another hour, and thus during the day we had rain and sunshine alternating very systematically indeed, and quite encouragingly.

The amount of water that had fallen barely sufficed to wet the thirsty earth, and it would therefore require just six such rainy days to give us water sufficient to commence our washing operations. Mr. Back's extensive researches into the science of astronomy enabled him to predict an astonishing amount of wet weather; at least such, he said, was *prognoxicated* by the *starring ferment*, that really the stars were looking so very wet and uncomfortable, that he could not but pity their condition, especially jolly old Aaron, with the belt. Shad had drunk a more than ordinary quantity of liquor that day, in commemoration, I suppose, of the beginning of the rainy season.

We were now well into the month of December. The rainy season usually commences about the middle of November, and continues almost without intermission until the latter part of February. The year previous it had rained for three months without cessation; now we had no rain. December passed away, and January had come, still the drought continued. Men and animals drooped, the earth had become baked, not a shrub, not a leaf, no, not even a blade of grass could be seen in any direction. A drier season had never been known in that region.

Shad had been sober for several days upon compulsion entirely. He could get no more liquor, not because the fiery draught was scarce, but for want of money to pay for it. My own funds were out, gone to liquidate our daily expenses, so that the prospect before us looked gloomy enough. I think, had it been our good fortune to have water, we should have made a very handsome sum out of our large heap of dirt. Without water, to separate the precious metal from the dirt, we could do nothing. About the 20th of January it rained nearly all the morning. "Hope told a flattering tale." Alas for us poor devils, the rain ceased at noon; this same half a day's rain cost Shad the only shirt he had for liquor. He said he felt morally certain the rainy season had set in *now*, and that he would have a regular jollification upon the strength of it, if it cost him his shirt, and it *did* cost him his shirt.

The season was now so far advanced that we could no longer hope for continuous rain, if it came at all; so I resolved, though with reluctance and after much deliberation, to abandon our *pile of gold* and make the best of my way back to San Francisco. It was all well enough that I should make a resolve of this description, but the principal part of the affair would be to carry it into effect. The *primum mobile*, the *sinews of war*, the *wherewith* must first be found before I could budge an inch. It was next to impossible to expect aid or counsel from poor Shad. He, good, susceptible soul, had fallen a willing victim to the artful blandishments of an ancient squaw, not so much on account of her great personal attractions as in consequence of her valuable possessions, which consisted of a dilapidated blanket and a keg of whiskey. I was quite charmed with the appearance of the squaw, she so strongly resembled a kangaroo; indeed it was quite a treat to see the pair together, it being problematical which was the most hideous, or the most beastly. I found it utterly useless to remonstrate with him; in fact, he never was in a fitting condition to understand me: so I made up my mind to leave him. Through the kindness of a friend, which was afterwards reciprocated, I was enabled to pay the few debts I had contracted, and to leave Columbia with a trifle of money, which, with economy, enabled me to reach San Francisco in due time.

Thus terminated my last mining adventure in the gold regions of California.

CHAPTER XVII.

THE VIGILANCE COMMITTEE.

The title of our chapter will bring up to the minds of all who visited California, during its early days, some startling recollections. The Vigilance Committee was the institution of that country, striking terror into all evil doers. Like all energetic associations, it was capable of being abused and sometimes ran into extremes, but its worst enemies cannot deny that it was the only thing which could suppress crime at the time it was in power.

Great mistakes are made in regard to this organization by most writers who have spoken of it. They have committed the very common error of judging of the institutions of one set of people by the standard of another. They have applied to California the same rule which would guide them in their judgment of an Atlantic State. In reality, however, there is no parallel between the two. The latter is inhabited by a population educated to regard the law as the paramount authority. The lawless are in the minority among them. Years of good government have taught the criminal to look upon the public authorities as his bitterest foes, and the honest man to regard them as his friends and protectors.

In California, however, every thing was the reverse of this. No sooner were her doors thrown open and her treasures disclosed, than people from every quarter of the globe thronged to her shores. Men of industrious habits and adventurous spirit went thither of course, as they always hasten to every new field of enterprise. The crowd of newcomers, however, was swelled by others of a far different character. Plunder was of course to be had, and the swindlers and desperadoes, who live by their wits, were quite as eager to visit the new country as were the honest miners who had come to wrench fortune from the flinty bowels of the earth by their brawny arms.

Villains from all parts of the world swarmed upon the new soil. Cunning sharpers from New England, desperate vagabonds from Texas, bogus men from the north-west, and reckless plunderers from the prairies hastened to California like crows to a corn-field. Mexico sent thither her sly robbers, Chili and Peru furnished their secret assassins. The penal colonies of Great Britain vomited their refuse upon this unhappy land, and even savage pirates from the Eastern Archipelago found their way to El Dorado. The territory numbered among her inhabitants accomplished thieves, burglars and cut-throats from every civilized and barbarous country within reach, men who had been familiar with courts and jails, and all punishments short of death.

It may readily be understood what a state of society existed there. The laws of the United States were, by a figure of speech, said to be in force over the new territory. Really, however, they were as impotent as they are in a village of Blackfeet among the Rocky Mountains. The officers of the law were utterly powerless. Rarely did they attempt to assert their authority, and when they did make the effort, they signally failed. The only law recognized there was that of the strongest. The correct aim, the steady hand, the strong arm were the only protectors of a Californian in those days. He might as well lean upon a wilted blade of grass as upon the legal authorities.

This condition of affairs afforded a fine harvest to the amiable gentlemen who had come hither to practice their professions. Robberies and murders became every-day occurrences, of no more importance than an assault and battery on election day. The most daring outrages were every where committed with impunity. Unoffending men were shot down and pillaged in broad daylight; shops were broken open; haciendas were stormed;—in short, the country was in a state of siege, and the blackguards were in the ascendent.

At this critical period, some of the settlers fortunately recollected a similar state of affairs in the country between the Mississippi and the Alleghanies, and the sharp but effective remedy which was then applied. They remembered how organized bands of robbers had infested the states and territories of the Mississippi Valley, how judges and constables and sheriffs had been connected with these infamous associations, how justice was perpetually defrauded of her dues, because juries composed of members of the same villainous fraternity could easily be packed; and how, finally, the honest portion of the community, exasperated beyond endurance by these repeated villainies, took the law in their own hands, and remorselessly hung and shot all the desperadoes who fell into their power, with the ultimate effect of restoring peace and good order.

The same evil demanded the same remedy. The Vigilance Committee was organized. It was composed of the best men in San Francisco, men who would have been the most zealous supporters of the law, had there been any law to support; men of firmness and resolution who were determined to have peace and security at all hazards. It was not exactly a secret society, but some sort of privacy was necessary to be observed. Were its agents generally known, not only would they be marked out for the secret vengeance of the vermin they were hunting down, but their vigilance would be more easily evaded, and the operations of the committee crippled.

The most important question which occurred to the committee, at its very formation, was the disposition to be made of the criminals arrested by its agents. They had no prisons at their command, and had no time to devote to the tedious formalities of law proceedings. Ropes, however, were at their disposal, and even California had trees enough to answer their purposes, except San Francisco, where the pulleys upon hoisting beams which projected from the warehouses afforded a very convenient substitute. Their code, therefore, necessarily resembled Draco's. For graver crimes they hung their culprits, for minor offences they flogged them, rode them on rails, tarred and feathered them, and ordered them away from a settlement within a given time under penalty of sharper punishment. Their threats were generally punctually executed. Their principle was that of Mr. Carlyle—to get rid of rascality by exterminating the rascals.

The results of the proceedings of this committee were beneficial in the highest degree. Before its establishment, it was dangerous to walk the streets of San Francisco in broad daylight; after it had been in operation for a short time, that city became as safe as any upon the other sea-board. They retained their authority until a State government had been formed, its officers duly appointed, and its sovereignty proclaimed; after which they laid it down. Whatever may be thought of the organization, no one can accuse it of intentional injustice. Hasty they may occasionally have been, but deliberately wrong, never. The best tribute that could be paid to their honesty and efficiency was the general apprehension of the people on the occasion of the charge just alluded to. They dreaded the establishment of a government of law, and generally preferred the irresponsible action of the committee. It is also a well ascertained fact that California has never been so orderly as it was under their rule. Immediately upon their resignation, the rogues began to breathe more freely, and crime to increase....

We have already said that this committee has been harshly judged and unjustly condemned by persons who were imperfectly or not at all acquainted with the facts in the case. These very men, however, recognize the necessity and acknowledge the benefits of the Holy Vehm. They can see plainly enough that the robber barons "who spared not man in their anger nor woman in their lust," who were a curse and a nuisance to all honest people, needed to be struck suddenly and without remedy by some invisible hand, which they could neither escape by flight, intimidate by threats, nor bribe with money.

They cannot understand, however, that the plebeian scoundrels of California required the same sharp and summary punishments which were needed for the rascally noblemen of the dreaded Red Land of Westphalia. It is very easy for people who sit by their comfortable firesides and look out upon well-fed policemen patrolling the streets, conspicuous by their glittering star, to descant upon the beauties of law and order. The man, however, who has just been knocked down and robbed in San Francisco by a vagabond who cannot be brought to justice, has not so clear a perception of the necessity of resorting to a tribunal which is powerless to punish, or of appealing to a constable who is equally unable to protect him from injury. These things have a relative, not an actual value; they are, or, perhaps I ought to say, they were worthless in California. A cockney traveler might as well take a London policeman to Sebastopol to prevent the Cossacks from taking liberties with his sacred person.

The main thing every where to be attained is order, that honest men may do their work in peace and quietness. If law gives them this, well and good. Law must be supported. If law is powerless, then the rifle, or the knife, or the rope must take its place. In so unsettled a state of society, as that which existed in California at the time of which we are speaking, the first thing is to strike terror into the ruffians. That must be done, let the cost be what it may. After the power of the honest man is established on a firm basis, then it is time enough to organize courts of law.

The quiet and honest settlers of California were fully convinced of the necessity of this committee, and zealously supported it. Indeed, the committee rarely acted alone. Almost always the citizens were called in, and had as much to say as the members of this self-constituted tribunal upon the case in hand. They only took the initiative; they saw that the scoundrels did not escape; the public did the rest.

As for the thieves, robbers and rascals of every grade, they entertained a wholesome terror of this energetic organization. When one of them received his orders to quit a certain place, he did not dare to disobey. He knew that unless he did what he was commanded, his punishment was inevitable. The committee was as inexorable as destiny itself.

I have no time to go into the examination of the arguments advanced against such an institution as this. A glance at one or two must suffice. It has been said that the committee was irresponsible, and that it is highly dangerous to entrust the power of life and death to irresponsible hands. In truth, however, the committee was not irresponsible. It sprang from the people, and though not formally elected by them, was nevertheless tacitly acknowledged. All its power resulted from the fact that it was a genuine exponent of public opinion, a faithful executor of the public will. The moment it failed fairly to represent the people, that moment its days were numbered. The members of the committee knew perfectly well that the same fate which they decreed to the culprits who fell into their hands, awaited them, should they ever become dangerous to the people.

Again, they have been accused of haste and cruelty in their operations. We have already said something on this head. Perhaps, however, it may be well to speak more directly to this charge. The necessity of punishment must be granted. There is no other mode of preserving order. Now, it must be remembered that California was then really in a state of anarchy, though nominally under the government of the United States. Every body did that which was right in his own eyes, or rather what his inclination prompted him to attempt. The consequence was, as we have already said, that murders and robberies were every-day occurrences. Life and property were wholly unprotected. In this state of affairs the vigilance committee took the matter up, and determined to regulate affairs. What were they to do with a criminal once caught? To take bail for him, and let him run till a certain course of regular formalities could be gone through with? That would have been an extremely judicious proceeding. The escaped scoundrel would have committed further depredations, and, in all probability, the most conspicuous of the committee would have fallen victims to his vengeance. It was necessary, therefore, to try him at once, or else let him go scot-free. The trial over, and conviction obtained, the sentence, whatever it might be, required to be immediately executed, because they had no place of safe-keeping for him. If exile was decreed, he was forthwith drummed out of the settlement; if he was to be hung, the rope was immediately provided. There was no help for it; unless justice were summary, it was null.

As for the charge of cruelty, it must be acknowledged that the code of the vigilance committee was severe. They hung for many offences which, in the Eastern States, can only deprive a man of his liberty. This also was a matter of necessity. Such severity was requisite to strike terror into the lawless vagabonds who infested the newly settled country. Besides, it was doing no more than was done in civilized, refined, enlightened England less than fifty years ago. Indeed, the vigilance committee were more merciful than the authorities of that realm, who hung a rogue for stealing a hat. It was only when a robbery was attended with circumstances of peculiar atrocity that they resorted to this extreme punishment.

Allowance must also be made for the state of feeling among the people in regard to capital punishment. It did not inflict such a shock upon them as it does on the inhabitants of an old, regularly governed country. Life was held very cheap there; it was taken upon the slightest provocation. Every man went armed, and weapons were resorted to at the commencement of a fray. The dry goods man, who measured out calico behind his counter, waited on his customers with a pair of revolvers stuck in his belt. The customers, wild, savage looking men, leaned upon their rifles or played with their bowie-knives while making their bargain. The purchase completed, the buyer threw down his leathern bag of gold dust, the seller weighed out the proper quantity and returned the rest. Should a dispute arise, few words were interchanged; arms were immediately appealed to, and the question was speedily settled. It is but fair, however, to say that, during these early days, the regular traders had but few difficulties with the miners, arising from attempts to defraud. Clearly, such a state of society cannot be judged by the same rule which applies to a settled and orderly community. A scene which I witnessed at Sacramento will probably give my readers a better idea of the mode of proceeding adopted by the vigilance committee, than any lengthened description of mere generalities.

A man who had recently returned from the mines, and was on his way to his home on the Atlantic coast, arrived in Sacramento one morning, and put up at the Orleans hotel. He had been quite successful in his labors, and brought in a goodly quantity of gold dust, a portion of which only he had deposited; the rest he carried about his person for current expenses. Elated with his good fortune, he could not refrain from boasting of his skill and judgment, and the excellent results he had obtained. He exhibited sundry little leather bags, and picked out nuggets remarkable for size or for oddity of form, which he exhibited freely to all the inmates of the house. He had one irregular mass of gold, which, to his fancy, resembled a race-horse. Another jagged, shapeless lump, he conceived to be a perfect likeness of Mr. Polk, whom he greatly admired, and this he declared his intention of having made into a breast-pin. He talked largely of the great things he would do with his money when he reached home, and, in the excess of his liberality, "treated the crowd" to innumerable cock-tails and smashes.

Two men, who were unknown to the people of the hotel, seemed particularly interested in the history of his exploits, and professed to have acquired a high regard for him personally, during their brief acquaintance. They swore he was a trump, that such a good fellow deserved to make money, and professed to rejoice in his success as greatly as though it had been their own. They too, they said, had just come in from the mines, where they had made a few ounces, though nothing like what our friend had secured. They were so exhilarated by his good fortune that they vowed they would return and try their luck again. They had come down with the intention of going home, but they did not like to be beaten by any one, so they would just "knock around" the city a little, have some fun, and go back to the mines the next day. Our friend was "such a devilish good fellow," that they were proud to have made his acquaintance, and would enjoy their frolic ten-fold if they could only prevail upon him to accompany them.

Their proposition was accepted. Success and "red-eye" had rendered him more than usually confiding, and the three strolled away, amid the laughter of the crowd, reeling, hiccoughing, and swearing eternal friendship. They rambled off to a back street, engaged in the same interesting conversation. Suddenly one of the companions of our hero disengaged himself from his arm, slipped behind him, and with a billet gave him a tremendous blow upon the head, which knocked him bleeding upon the pavement. He was stunned only for a moment, and the blow seemed to have sobered him. He began to struggle, when his other newly found friend joined in the assault. The two together belabored him severely over the head till he lay senseless and motionless upon the pavement. Thinking they had quieted him for ever, they proceeded to rifle his pockets, and soon stripped him of every thing valuable he had about his person. They then made off with their booty.

Strange as it may sound to my reader, this outrage was perpetrated about three o'clock on a summer afternoon. Some persons in the neighborhood witnessed the whole affair, and immediately gave the alarm. The vigilance committee, ever on the alert, were soon in pursuit, and the scoundrels were captured a short distance from the outskirts of the city. The news spread with great rapidity, and soon a large crowd had collected. When I reached the scene of action, the members of the committee were escorting the culprits to a little grove of stunted oaks which stood upon the outskirts of the town. There was an expression of calm determination on the faces of the committee, of angry excitement on those of the rest of the crowd. Furious cries of "hang them!" burst from the mob, but did not seem to excite or ruffle the chief actors in this terrible drama, who went about their duties with great system and deliberation. As for the criminals themselves, a more villainous pair of faces it was never my fortune to look upon. Low brows, heavy features, and cold steel-gray eyes, gave them the expression with which Cruikshanks has pictured Sykes in his illustrations of Oliver Twist. They were Australian convicts, brutal wretches, whose hands were red with blood.

A jury was immediately empanneled by order of the committee, one of whom acted as judge. "Fellow-citizens," said he, "these men have been accused of perpetrating an atrocious crime within the limits of this city. We are now ready to give them a fair trial. Those gentlemen who witnessed the outrage will now come forward and give in their testimony!"

The culprits were made to confront the jury, guarded by members of the Vigilance Committee. Several citizens came forward and stated what they had seen, and others from the hotel identified the prisoners as the men who went off with the unlucky miner. They also recognized the bags and the nuggets which were taken from them as the same which had been exhibited at the hotel. As for the wounded man, he was too badly hurt to testify.

The case was fairly made out against them, the jury gave in their verdict, and the judge formally inquired what the convicts had to say why sentence should not be pronounced upon them. They muttered out a few unintelligible words, when with a clear loud voice, he said: "Prisoners, you have been found guilty of a murderous assault and robbery. You have had a fair trial, and the sentence of this court is that you be forthwith hung by the neck till you are dead! One hour will be granted for such religious exercises as you may desire. If there is any one present who is disposed to render these men any religious service, he is requested to come forward."

A man, who represented himself as a Methodist preacher, now advanced to the miserable men, said a few words to them in a low tone of voice, and then knelt down to pray beside them. During this part of the ceremony, the crowd stood silently by, and many took off their hats.

Presently the preacher rose and mingled with the crowd. A man advanced to the culprits and carefully pinioned their arms with a strong rope. At this stage of the proceedings, they seemed to be fully aroused to a sense of their danger. They looked around and seemed to scrutinize every face in the whole assembled multitude. Never shall I forget that mute, appealing gaze. It was useless; not a face in the whole crowd wore an aspect of mercy; but again arose the angry shout: "Hang them! hang them!" The judge now called out, "Gentlemen! the hour is up!" whereupon they were led to a tree and swung off. A few struggles and all was over. The crowd quietly dispersed; the excitement subsided, and an hour afterwards no one would have suspected that any thing unusual had happened.

Such proceedings as these—the absolute and inevitable certainty of punishment—produced order throughout the State. Indeed, it was the Vigilance Committee alone that ever has enforced obedience to law. The State's Attorney of San Francisco states that in four years *twelve hundred murders had been perpetrated, and only one of the criminals was convicted.* What wonder if some people still sigh for the days of the Vigilance Committee?

CHAPTER XVIII.

BODEGA.

Once more in San Francisco, I made preparations to return to the Atlantic States as rapidly as my health and dilapidated means would permit. Before leaving this pseudo Eldorado for ever and aye, I had a wish to see a celebrated grazing district, famed for its vast herds of horned cattle and wild horses; and so, having hired at an enormous price a sorry looking mule, like the knight of La Mancha mounted upon Rosinante, I sallied forth from San Francisco in search of new adventures. I took the high road along the bay towards Bodega, a small town situated upon the Pacific coast, 60 miles north-east from San Francisco. I had hardly cleared the suburbs of the city, when my mule began to exhibit qualities very far from respectable; as, for example, he would stop suddenly, hold down his head, plant his fore feet firmly, and reflect, I suppose, upon the proper moment to pitch me over his head. He had a very uncomfortable way too of throwing up his head, and more than once just grazed my nose; then he was so playful! jerking the bridle suddenly and casting his head round so as almost to reach my leg with his teeth. And, moreover, I judged him to be partial to botanical studies, from the fact of his taking every opportunity of pushing his way through the scrub bushes that lined the road, as if he thought the occasion favorable to scrape me off his back. I have never been very famous for my skill in equitation, nor have I ever been too anxious to intrust myself to the care and safe-keeping of other legs than my own, and I must acknowledge that when I discovered the little pleasing eccentricities already enumerated, I thought it would be most prudent to return; and would have done so, only that the devilish brute would not consent to take the back track; by which I mean that, when I attempted to turn his head homeward, he commenced such a series of circumgyratory evolutions that I remained long in doubt as to which of my limbs would remain unbroken when I *did* come to the ground, a catastrophe by no means far distant if he continued to spin around five minutes longer. I clung to the pummel of the Spanish saddle, however, with the gripe of a maniac, shouting wo! with an unction and vigor that I am sure contributed as much as any thing else towards stopping the incarnate devil in his mad career. Any person, to have seen my involuntary performances on this trying occasion, would most assuredly have pronounced me the best circus rider in the known world. I am favorably known at home as an even tempered, nay, as a good tempered person; but I verily believe I lost my temper here on this spot, not that I remember to have ever been profane, but I am sure I consigned the wretch to the safe-keeping of a nameless personage, with a particular request regarding the future disposition of his eyes and limbs. As I could do nothing better, I let him have his own way, and for the next hour or so we got along very well together, and I really began to think well of his muleship; when suddenly, and as if by magic, I found myself upon my back in the road, and the precious villain prancing and curveting within fifty feet of where I lay, as if in the very act of rejoicing that he had thrown me there. I had received a slight bruise upon one of my shoulders by the fall, a matter not deserving much attention, and was considering the best method of catching the atrocious robber, as he very deliberately walked up to me, and adjusted his position so that I could mount him again with ease, which I did without delay. Shortly after, we reached a Chinese encampment—all men, or at least I supposed so. They looked exactly alike in face and in dress. Two or three were assembled around a fire, the rest were gambling; those by the fire were engaged in cooking rats in an expeditious manner. I should think there might have been about a bushel of these animals altogether, and they were laid with their skins on, from time to time, upon a bed of hot embers to broil; it was a very primitive way of replenishing the larder! However, I did not dine with the celestials; I had an indistinct idea at the moment that the moon's relatives were exceedingly respectable, only something the filthiest. Without much further trouble or delay we arrived, towards midnight, at Bodega. My mule behaved like a trump during the latter part of the journey, but only after frolicking for about three quarters of an hour up and down a small stream upon our road, which his excellency insisted upon surveying, even from its source to its mouth.

Bodega contains not more than four hundred inhabitants, including "Digger" Indians, "niggers" and dogs, the last by far the most useful and most decent of the concern. The people of the town told me that the place was first settled by the Russians, but no vestiges remain of the original settlers to denote who or what they were. A very worthy man is the sole proprietor of the town now—he is an American; some years since resided in Valparaiso, where he married several bags of doubloons, a large lot of cattle, some fine horses, and a Chilian lady; removed to California and became the possessor of the town of Bodega, and a very large portion of the surrounding country. For my part, I could see nothing very seductive in Bodega, nothing that could keep me there a week. The country is almost destitute of timber, with here and there a woody knoll. The surface of the land is rolling, soil good, and well adapted for farming purposes. In fact, it is said to be the best grazing section in the State of California. Dense fogs prevail throughout the summer months; from these the earth receives a sufficient quantity of moisture to answer all the purposes of rain. An abundant crop of grass is produced, upon which vast herds of cattle and droves of horses are raised. The horned cattle are slaughtered in immense numbers, merely for their horns, hides and tallow.

Twelve miles south-east of Bodega is the little village of Petaluma, situated upon the margin of an extensive swamp or morass, through which a small stream winds its way to the bay of San Francisco. This morass is entirely overflowed during the winter. In the summer it becomes perfectly dry, and cracks open in every imaginable direction to the depth of twelve or fifteen feet, the crevices varying from one to eight inches in width. At an early period the Indians captured entire herds of horned cattle in the summer by driving them into this morass. If an animal attempts to cross this fissured spot he must assuredly break his legs. It is no uncommon occurrence daily to find three or four wild horses, and as many more horned cattle, vainly struggling to extricate their fractured limbs from the clefts and crevices in this death-dealing Golgotha. In this situation they are quickly dispatched by the Indians and others living in the vicinity, stripped of their hides, and the carcasses left for the birds of prey. Owing to certain preservative properties in the atmosphere, animal matter does not undergo decomposition in this region with the same degree of rapidity that it does in other sections of the Atlantic States in the same parallels of latitude, and it is not unusual to see the carcasses of slain animals upon this very morass, a month or more after they have fallen, in a good state of preservation, and without emitting, in any great degree, an offensive odor.

Upon my return to Bodega, I witnessed the punishment of an Indian boy for theft. This was the case: The boy had stolen a trifling sum from the house of an American, and being shortly after detected with the money in his possession, he was sentenced to expiate his offence in a very novel manner; and here I might with great propriety use the language of Lord Byron, the scene reminded me so strongly of the main incidents of his Mazeppa. A wild horse that had been caught with the lasso only the day before, was brought out, and the boy's person in an upright position securely strapped to his back. The boy thus bound, the horse was then freed from restraint by the men that held him, and with a cut from a whip, he bounded away with the speed and swiftness of an arrow shot from a bow. The race, however, was of short duration. He had scarcely accomplished the third of a mile, when he suddenly threw himself, and with frantic efforts endeavored to roll over and over, in order to rid himself of his burden. In these struggles, one of the boy's legs was literally crushed into a bloody mass. The violent exertions of the animal had so far exhausted his strength, that he was unable to rise. In this condition, we had time to come up and liberate the boy from his bonds, but not until the poor creature had ceased to breathe. He was quite dead, and another murder was to be added to the long list of California crimes. Horror-sticken and distressed at the scene of ruthless barbarity I had just witnessed, I made my way out of the village of Bodega, wondering if the good God would permit such an unparalleled atrocity to pass unpunished.

In returning, I took the road through the valleys of Sonoma and Napa to Benicia ; feeling fatigued and somewhat indisposed upon reaching the city of Benicia, I determined to rest there a day or two. Benicia contains about 1500 inhabitants, is 40 miles north-east from San Francisco, situated upon a branch of the Sacramento river. The city is regularly laid out on a gentle slope, rising from the water's edge to the hills in the rear. Benicia is a port of entry, contains an arsenal, a navy-yard, and extensive docks for repairing and refitting steamers. Ships of the largest class can come up to the wharves. It has been proposed to establish the seat of government of the State here. It must be by no means understood that I had traveled thus far upon my return without trouble from the antics and extravagances of my mule, being somewhat upon my guard, I more than once foiled him in his design of getting me off his back. I have seen vicious animals in my time, but never saw any thing to equal the cunning and malice of this one. It seemed as if he had been taught every thing that was bad, and being naturally vicious, had become by long practice more than a match for man. Desirous of examining more closely a singularly formed elevation some fifteen miles from Benicia, known as Monte Diabolo, I set out the third morning after my sojourn in Benicia to visit this famous mountain. Mounted upon my rascally mule, I had unfortunately suffered myself to be persuaded to wear a pair of Spanish spurs, having been assured that the fractious conduct of the mule heretofore was entirely owing to my not providing myself with these persuaders at the commencement of my journey. I had ridden barely the half of a mile, when the accursed animal was seized with a fiend-like desire to break my neck and his own too. With this commendable purpose in view, he began by taking short leaps forward, backward and sideways, varied every now and then by an effort to throw me over his head, by casting his hind legs high into the air, or in endeavoring to force me off by standing almost upright, and pawing the air with his fore feet. I maintained my seat with difficulty during these fiendish gambols, and plied him with the spurs. This settled the matter at once, for no sooner did I plunge the sharp rowels into his infernal sides, than he stood for a moment, as if to gather strength for a more mighty effort; then, dropping his head, he suddenly threw out his hind feet with such violence as to eject me from his back with an impetus that I am astonished did not crush every bone in my body, and kill me outright. As it was, my left leg only was broken. The mule, demon as he was, seemed to exult in his misdeeds, and to be well content with the (to him) triumphant termination of the contest; at least I judged so, from his sounding the trumpet of victory long and loud; he brayed incessantly for an hour. My leg was broken just above the ankle, and whenever I moved gave me exquisite pain. What to do I did not know; I could not move. I was somewhat comforted, however, by reflecting that I should not lie in this helpless condition long. I was on the highway, and some traveler must pass soon. I shouted with all the voice I had left; pain and agony had weakened me so much, that I feared death would ensue before my situation could be known. At length I attempted to drag myself upon my hands and knees towards Benicia, then less than a mile distant. In the effort, the agony I endured caused me to faint. I know not how long I lay in this death-like condition. When I again returned to consciousness, I found myself in bed, with my broken limb confined between splints, after having been properly set by a surgeon. Many weary days and nights were passed upon a bed of sickness. I received every attention from the kind people into whose hands I had fallen. These good Samaritans had found me insensible by the wayside, my mule standing within ten feet of me, very gravely contemplating his handiwork, afterwards suffering himself to be led back to Benicia, without making the slightest demonstration of discontent. As soon as my new friends discovered the cause of my accident, it was proposed to shoot the mule forthwith. To this summary disposition of the malignant brute I objected, not from any desire to save his worthless carcass, but from a wish to return him to his more worthless owner in San Francisco, whom I had some hope the animal would cripple for life upon some future day. I therefore requested my friends to have him returned to his owner by the first opportunity that offered.

My most constant attendant was an old negro named Ben. A better nurse I could not have had than this same old fellow. As he was quite an original, I will describe him. Ben was about four feet six inches in height, very thin and very black; his grandfather must have been a chimpanzee—I feel quite sure of that, because his features were precisely those of an ancient baboon; his age might be about fifty or fifty-five, and at an earlier day he may have had a nose, I doubt it, though; at any rate he had none when I saw him. No! not a bit. It had disappeared altogether. The wool grew within an inch of his eye-brows, and he had but one eye. Ordinarily and for economy's sake, Ben was very simply attired in canvas pantaloons and the remnant of a red woolen shirt—disdaining hat and shoes, except upon great occasions and State celebrations; then, indeed, Ben shone conspicuous in all the glory of an immensely high bell-crowned white hat, with a narrow rim and a broad green ribbon to match, a tall, stiff shirt collar that reached his ears, a military stock, tightly buckled around his neck, which effectually prevented the wearer from looking downward, a whitish looking something that had been worn for at least seven years as an overcoat by a tall, stout man, now served Ben in the capacity of a dress coat; to be sure he had "curtailed its fair proportions" by cutting off one and a half feet of the skirts, six inches of the sleeves and a good large piece of the collar. It was a nice garment. A pair of breeches so tight that he slept in them upon occasions when he had used much exercise, for the simple reason that he could not get them off without greatly endangering their respectable appearance; boots large and somewhat dilapidated, of course the legs of the tights could not be drawn over the boots, therefore they were tucked inside. But the crowning glory of the entire outer man was a broad, shining, black leather belt, drawn so tightly around his waist, that he breathed at times short and sharp.

To Ben's many other great talents must be added his very great proficiency in music. He performed very spiritedly indeed upon the bass drum, and when necessary, could do the jingling upon the triangle. But his forte was the fife, and it was a pleasing sight to see him upon a gala day, rigged as described, lugging a huge drum buckled to his breast bone, thrashing away with both hands as if his life depended upon the amount of confusion he created. Suddenly he would cease, and drawing the fife from the depths of his breeches pocket, would favor the procession or company with an air from "Norma," or from somewhere else. Heroic Ben! can I ever forget the day when, attired in all his bravery, tall hat, big coat, old boots, bright belt, long drum, short fife and all, he hobbled past the house wherein I lay, followed by all the boys, girls and dogs in the place? It was some saint's day, and the Mexicans had hired Ben as chief musician to aid with such music as he had on hand in doing proper honor to his saintship; and he did it, too, much to the admiration of every one within hearing. No! I shall never forget that day; I think the sight hastened the recovery of my health and strength.

At the end of five weeks, the doctor told me I could travel without danger to my leg, provided I was careful; accordingly I took passage on board of the steamer New World for San Francisco, and, with Ben as my body-guard, reached that city late in the evening of the same day without any further accident. I immediately put myself under the care of an able physician, and in a very short time experienced no inconvenience from my now perfect leg. As to Ben, he would not leave me, and in fact he made himself so necessary to my comfort that I was quite loth to part with him. He was a good servant, a good nurse, and honest as far as circumstances would permit; but he would get liquor to drink some how; no matter in what shape it came, Ben must have liquor; buy, beg, borrow or steal, have it he would. I have known him to drink the doctor's prescriptions, in consequence of their having a small quantity of brandy in them; but for this failing I think I should have brought him back with me to the Atlantic States; as it was, I parted from him only upon the day that I sailed for home.

CHAPTER XIX.

THE DIGGER INDIANS AND NEGROES.

Of all the aborigines that are known to travelers within the limits of the western continent, the Digger Indians are certainly the most filthy and abominable. A worse set of vagabonds cannot be found bearing the human form. They come into the world and go from it to as little purpose as other carnivorous animals. Their chief characteristics are indolence and gluttony. Partially wrapped in filthy rags, with their persons unwashed, hair uncombed and swarming with vermin, they may be seen loitering about the kitchens and slaughter-houses awaiting with eager gaze to seize upon and devour like hungry wolves such offal or garbage as may be thrown to them from time to time. Grasshoppers, snails and wasps are favorite delicacies with them, and they have a peculiar relish for a certain little animal, which the Bible tells us greatly afflicted the Egyptians in the days of Pharaoh. The male Digger never hunts—he is too lazy for this; he usually depends upon the exertions of his squaw to provide something or other to satisfy the cravings of hunger.

The term Digger has been applied to these Indians in consequence of their method of procuring their food. The grasshopper or cricket of California is one of their favorite messes. They capture these insects by first digging a pit in the ground, and then forming a wide circle round it which is gradually narrowed. In this manner they drive the insects to the pit and there capture them. After having secured their prey, the next thing is to prepare it for food. This is accomplished either by baking the grasshoppers in the fire or drying them in the sun, after which the Diggers pulverize them. The epicures among them crush service-berries into a jam and thoroughly incorporate the pulverized insects with the pulpy mass to which they have reduced the fruit. Others mix their cricket meal with parched sunflower seed, but this is an advance in civilization and in the luxuries of the table, which is made by very few of them. They obtain the young wasps by burning the grass, which exposes the nests and enables them to grub in the earth for this delicacy.

Acorns are also a favorite article of diet with these wretched creatures. In California, this fruit is larger and more palatable than with us, and it has the merit of being a cleaner kind of food than that which usually satisfies the Digger's hunger. Rude as these people are, they have sense enough to observe that all years are not equally productive in these nuts, and foresight sufficient to lay in a good stock during the plentiful years. They pound them up, mix them with wild fruit, and make their meal into a sort of bread. They are said to resort to a stratagem to obtain the acorns in greater abundance. There is a bird in California, called, from his habits, the carpenteir or carpenter. He busies himself in making holes in the redwood trees and filling them with acorns. When a Digger finds a tree stocked in this manner, he kindles a fire at its base, (so the story goes,) and keeps it up till the tree falls, when he helps himself to the acorns.

Grass-seed constitutes another portion of their diet, and this is gathered by the women, who use for the purpose, two baskets, one shaped like a shield, the other deep and provided with a handle. With the shield the top of the grass is brushed and the seed shaken down into the deep basket. This also is made into bread.

It is commonly supposed that these Indians belong to a single tribe. This, however, I think is doubtful. They are scattered over a wide extent of country, being found far to the north, among the Utahs. Those upon the frontier usually call themselves Shoshonees or Snakes, while some claim to be Utahs. Their skin is nearly as dark as that of the negro. Indeed they greatly resemble the African in color and general appearance. They are distinguished from him chiefly by their aquiline noses, their long hair and their well-shaped feet. The southern Diggers have a lighter complexion, being not so dark as a mulatto.

It is reported on good authority that Captain Sutter, the first settler on the Sacramento, at whose fort (the present site of Sacramento) gold was first discovered, employed these people to build his fort for him. He paid them in tin coin of his own invention, upon which was stamped the number of days the holder had worked. This was taken at his "store" for articles of merchandise, such as dry goods, &c. He fed his field Indians upon the offal of slaughtered animals and the bran sifted from ground wheat. The latter was boiled in large iron kettles; and then placed in wooden troughs from which they scooped it out with their hands. They are said to have eaten it, poor as it was, with great relish, and it was no doubt more palatable and wholesome than their customary diet.

These Indians are inveterate gamblers, and when they have been so fortunate as to obtain clothing, they are almost sure to gamble it away before they stop. Their game is carried on as follows. A number sit cross-legged on the ground in a circle, and they are then divided into two parties, each of which has two head players. A ball is passed rapidly from hand to hand along the whole of one party, while the other attempts to guess in what hand it is. If successful, it counts one for the guessing party towards the game. If unsuccessful, it counts one in favor of the opposite party. The count is kept with sticks. All the while this is going on, they grunt in chorus, swinging their bodies to keep time with their grunts. The articles staked are placed in the centre of the ring. When they once get excited in play, they never stop so long as they have any thing to stake. After getting through with their money, their trinkets and their provisions, they stake their clothes and keep on gambling till they reduce themselves to the costume of Adam.

The fate of these poor creatures is involved in no uncertainty. They must melt away before the white man like snow before a spring sun. They are too indolent to work, too cowardly to fight. When pinched by the severity of hunger, and unable to procure their customary filthy diet, they are driven to the settlements, where they steal if they can, and do a little labor if they must. No sooner, however, have they procured the means of satisfying their immediate wants, than they abandon the employment offered them and relapse into their customary indolent habits. Of course, it can only be while labor is in such great demand as it now is, that they can secure even this temporary employment. When hands become abundant in that country, the laboring white man, the Chinese or the negro will monopolize all the work. The Indian then will be confined to thieving for a livelihood, and that is something which the Californians will not permit. Some of these miserable people have been cruelly butchered by the whites for indulging their propensity to make free with other people's property. They cannot fight for their plunder, and consequently they must suffer as patiently as they can whatever penalty is inflicted. If the fierce warlike tribes of the north could not oppose the march of civilization, how easily will these poor weak children of the south be crushed under its advancing wheels!

In Marysville, passing by one of the slaughter-houses, I saw a collection of about twenty of these wretches waiting for the offal. They were in the habit of presenting themselves regularly every morning at the same place and at the same hour to gather the refuse of the slaughtering establishment. The proprietors rather encouraged these visiters than otherwise, for the same reason that the turkey-buzzard's visits are so acceptable to the denizens of most of our southern cities—they serve the purpose of scavengers so admirably. On this particular occasion, however, one of the proprietors seemed not so well satisfied, from the fact of his having detected one or two of these "Diggers" in the very act of stealing some choice pieces of beef. A stalwart Tennesseean and his son were the proprietors. The father was a very stout man, and more than a match for fifty of these poor miserable devils; fond of whiskey, an inveterate swearer, and withal, when excited, as was then the case, dangerous. As soon as the theft was discovered the eldest Tennesseean seized a meat-axe, and with a tremendous oath threatened to immolate the entire tribe, or, to use his own quaint but profane language, to "populate hell three deep with the damned thieving Digger Indians in less than no time." This was said to his son, a good natured young man who was using his best endeavors to prevent his father from putting his terrible threat into execution. Happily for the Indians, they had sufficient time to get out of reach of the enraged man, and make good their escape with the stolen meat. The butcher's scheme for populating the infernal regions was to my mind quite original, to say the least of it, and notwithstanding the impiety of the thing, I could not refrain from laughing. It afterwards became a matter of grave consideration how he would accomplish an undertaking of this description, without first having recourse to some actual measurement, the better to determine the amount of feet and inches required for each separate body. I think he must have been something of a surveyor, and had already measured the area contained within the dominions of the evil one; how else could he name the precise depth of "Diggers" he intended to furnish? Our worthy butcher, it must be conceded, understood geometry, as "three deep" distinctly implies length, breadth and thickness. The only true difficulty in the whole thing was the specified period of its performance. I understand what is meant by "no time" very well, but cannot say I am so confident as to the meaning and intent of the phrase "in less than no time." I dare say though some very short period of time is intended, and if time and opportunity serves, upon some future day I will make the inquiry of the Tennesseean or his son (I should prefer the latter) what it really means.

There are comparatively few negroes in this new State. Most of those who are found here have emigrated from the northern and eastern States in the capacity of cooks and stewards of vessels. They are in the same situation as their brethren in New York and Massachusetts, slaves to no single individual but to the entire community. Like free negroes every where else, they inhabit the worst parts of the towns in California, and live commonly in characteristic filth and degradation.

There are a few blacks from the South, and these have been brought out here as slaves. It is true that on their arrival here they have the power of claiming their freedom; but such is their attachment to their masters that this is rarely done. Instances have occurred in which they have been enticed away by meddling abolitionists, but, disgusted with a freedom which was of no value to them, they have been eager to return again to their masters. Several cases of this kind have come under my own observation.

I was personally acquainted with a New Orleans sea-captain and ship-owner, who had a very likely negro man named Joe. This slave had acted as his special servant for many years, and had made two or three voyages with him between Shanghai and San Francisco. His conduct was entirely unobjectionable, and his duties were always promptly and efficiently discharged. Indeed, the captain informed me that, though he had reared Joe, he never had occasion to whip him for any offence. Others had observed the admirable traits of the negro, and several persons had attempted to buy him, offering extraordinary prices; but his master, having the highest appreciation of his qualities and a strong personal attachment for him, positively refused to part with him on any terms. At last, however, Joe deserted the vessel. An abolitionist had persuaded him to leave his master; and a short while thereafter he married a Mexican woman—a sort of half-breed—and went off to the mines, near Campo Seco. But he found his freedom unprofitable and troublesome. While in his legitimate station he had always had an easy time, plenty of food and an abundance of clothing. He had also accumulated two or three hundred dollars, which had been given him by his master, and others, for extra services. Not long after his marriage with the Mexican woman, his money disappeared. He became penniless, ragged, dejected, and, as a last resort, determined to return to San Francisco, beg his master's pardon, and, if possible, reinstate himself in the favor of one who had always been his friend. He did return, presented himself as a suppliant before his master, told him that he had been persuaded to leave, that he was sorry for having done so, and now wished to enter his service again, promising unwavering faithfulness in the future. The master regarded him with a steady gaze until he had finished his story, and then, in a distinct and dispassionate tone, said to him: "You had no cause for leaving me; I had always treated you well. Now you may go; I don't want you any longer." At the conclusion of these words, the negro dropped in despair at his master's feet, and wept like a child. Moved by the sincerity of the negro's repentance, and having duly considered the extenuating circumstances of the case, the master overlooked his estrangement, set him to work and never had the least difficulty with him afterwards. Of his Dulcina, whom it seems he had married in a Laguna dance-house, I know nothing, except the information I gained from Joe himself, that she left him as soon as his money was gone.

One more instance, and I have done with the negroes. A gentleman and three of his slaves, from the western part of North Carolina, had been mining about two years, near Quartzburg, in Mariposa county. Their efforts having been crowned with success, the master concluded to return home, and speaking to his slaves of his intention, he told them that they were at liberty to remain in California, where their freedom would not be disturbed, and where they would be entitled to the entire proceeds of their labor. To this they replied that the abolitionists had told them that long before, and after detailing several attempts to decoy them from their owner, and signifying their unwillingness to remain in California, they concluded by requesting their master to take them with him. He consented, paid their passage, and they all returned home in the same vessel.

The applicability of slave labor to the soil of Southern California is now becoming a theme of discussion in that region, and it is probable that the experiment will one day be tried. Indeed, the propriety of dividing the State into Northern and Southern California has already occupied the attention of the legislature; and while it is generally admitted that the people are about equally divided upon the measure, it is universally conceded that, in case of its adoption, the southern portion will establish the laws and institutions of Virginia and Louisiana.

CHAPTER XX.

ARE YOU GOING TO CALIFORNIA?

In the preceding chapters it has been my purpose to impart such information as would lead my reader to a correct knowledge of the present condition of things in California, and to aid him in deciding whether he will emigrate to that country, or content himself in the Atlantic States. I have endeavored (in a very brief and feeble manner, it is true) to purge the films from his eyes, that he might see the country in its true light. I have told him of the distorted and exaggerated stories which have been circulated concerning it; of its barren soil, and unfavorable seasons; of the seeming incompleteness of nature, and the paucity of resources of employment therein; of its scanty productions, and dependence upon importations for all kinds of provisions and merchandise; of the expensiveness of living, and the extraordinary obstacles which lie in the way of prosecuting business with success; of the unprecedented number of mishaps and accidents, and the losses and perils to be apprehended from fire and water; of the lack of scenery, and the disagreeable consequences of the weather; of the inefficiency of the laws, and the anarchical state of society; of the breaches of faith between man and wife—of the almost utter disregard of the marriage relation, and the unexampled debauchery and lewdness of the community; of the contrariety of opinions which prevail, and the continual disputes and disturbances which arise in consequence of the heterogeneousness of the population; of the servile employments to which learned and professional men have to resort for the means of subsistence, and the thousands of penniless vagabonds who wander about in misery and dejection; of the dissipated and desperate habits of the people, and the astounding number of suicides and murders; of the incessant brawls and tumults, and the popularity of dueling; of the arbitrary doings of mobs, and the supremacy of lynch-law; of the general practice of carrying deadly weapons, and the contempt that is shown for human life; of the great difficulty of securing reliable titles to landed property, and the fatal rencounters with the squatters; of the bacchanalian riots by day, and the saturnalian revels at night; of the perfidy and delinquency of public functionaries, and the impossibility of electing an honest man to office; of the sophistication of provisions, and the filthy fare in hotels and restaurants; of the untrustworthy character of business men, and the frauds and stratagems practiced in almost every transaction; of the contemning of religious sentiments, and the desecration of the Sabbath; of the incendiaries in the cities, and the banditti in the mountains; of the alarming depravity of the adolescent generation—of the abominable dissoluteness of many of the women—the infamous vices of the men, and the flagitious crimes against nature. I have spoken freely of all these things; and now what else shall I say? Is it necessary that I should defile still more paper with these detestable truths? Can any one be still in a state of indecision about going to California? I am aware that the public mind has been somewhat undecided upon this subject, and I have essayed to give it the proper turn, or restore it to its accustomed equilibrium. I have spread before my reader a combination of facts, and have related events which occurred under my own observation. There are scores of other topics which might be brought in to give strength to my general argument; but I dislike to tax the patience of the reader with such a prolonged catalogue of unwholesome realities.

It was my intention to dwell somewhat at length upon a variety of subjects of interest, but the space which I assigned to myself is already nearly filled up, so that I find I shall be compelled to abandon this design and bring these desultory remarks to a close. It would, however, be a neglect for which I would not readily excuse myself, were I to pass over the subject of the Pacific Railroad without note or comment. It is agitating the public mind too deeply, and it is too intimately connected not only with the prosperity of our Pacific coast, but also with that of the whole nation, to be lightly regarded; and as some point in California must be its terminus, if common sense is to guide us in selecting its course, a work on that country must necessarily take it into account.

The necessity of this important national highway is too strongly impressed upon the minds of the thinking people of this nation, to be easily lost sight of. Some erroneous opinions, however, are entertained in regard to the objects of the road by many who warmly advocate it. It is supposed by a few that California is to contribute some wonderful benefits to it, and some few even go so far as to suppose that she can support it. This is very absurd, as the previous chapters have, we hope, clearly explained.

California certainly will contribute something to the support of this great enterprise, but cannot, by any means, constitute the chief inducement to its construction. Her gold will of course come more rapidly, readily and safely across the continent than around Cape Horn. In this respect, the saving to the consignees on the Atlantic coast will be very great, and will be represented by three items: saving of time, saving in the interest of money, and saving in consequence of the diminution of the risks of transportation. A glance at our table of casualties by sea, in a former chapter, will show how great the last named saving promises to be. That on the interest of money will also be great. It requires about three weeks to send from California by the shortest existing route to New Orleans, while, by the railroad, that city will be but a few days' distant from San Francisco or San Diego. Allowing a week to be occupied in the trip, the saving in this item will amount to a half a month, and as a million is often brought in a single cargo, this is no trifle. At six per cent. per annum, it would amount to twenty-five hundred dollars on each shipment. The item of time will be sufficiently appreciated by the mercantile reader without comment from us.

These, however, are not the only benefits which the road may expect to derive directly from California. Much of the British commerce, which now finds its way to that distant region by the long routes, will go thither by the more direct and expeditious way of the new road. A way commerce will also inevitably spring up and there will be a cordon of settlements and towns stretching across a wilderness which years of ordinary immigration would be required to fill up. Branch roads would also soon start from the main trunk to various important regions along the route. The Santa Fe trade and the commerce of the prairies generally would soon seek this as its natural channel. The emigration to California would also largely benefit the road. This is likely to be large for some time to come, and the return tide would also contribute to increase the pecuniary revenue of this great national enterprise.

To California it would be of the greatest service, and the enlargement of the resources of that State would of course increase those of the improvement which causes the beneficial change. The country would then be settled from the east as well as from the west, and the gold of the Sierra Nevada would speedily be brought into market.

These advantages, considerable as they are, really form but a very small portion of the inducements to the construction of this important work. The great and important revenues of the road will come from far beyond the limits of the State. The enormous commerce of Eastern Asia and its Archipelago, which has enriched every nation that ever secured it, will then flow over our country leaving its golden sands behind it. China will send its teas, Amboyna its spices, Java its tin, Japan its copper, through our dominions. No commercial manœuvring, no diplomatic juggles can divert this mighty trade from its natural course. There is a destiny in commerce, as well as in other things, and fate seems determined to pour the riches of the world into our lap. If, in former times, the slow caravans which conveyed the treasures of the east to western ports, left wealth behind them, wherever their footprints were seen, though vexed by Tartar and by Arab plunderers, how much more benefit is likely to be derived from a rapid and safe transit through a civilized nation, ready, eager and able to add their quota to the stream of wealth?

We must not forget, also, that this eastern commerce is greater and more important than it ever was. Our efforts have unsealed Japan, and before long we shall be reaping the fruits of our enterprise in that quarter. Australia, too, is now ready to add her gold to a commerce already immensely valuable. China must open her doors still wider, for the world will knock loudly at them. Nor is this all. The whole trade of the western coast of South America must change its course. A Pacific capital is destined to absorb it. The whaling fleets of the Pacific will not have the stormy passage around Cape Horn to dread, but another New Bedford will look greasily upon the western ocean. The fur trade also will change its course. Oregon will furnish it with a port of departure, California with a permit of entry. Siberia itself may divide its trade between San Francisco and St. Petersburg. We seem to be on the point of taking the position which China has always claimed, and of becoming the true centre of the world, at least so far as commerce is concerned.

I believe it is now generally admitted that the Southern route is the most practicable—that it is the most level, the most fertile, the best watered, the best timbered, and that the climate through which it runs is the only one that is favorable at all seasons of the year. I have conversed with several gentlemen who passed over the various routes on their way to California, and they informed me that the mountainous parts of the northern routes are usually blocked up during the winter with immense drifts of snow, which lie upon the ground to the depth of from forty to fifty feet—sometimes much deeper. Those who traveled over the northern routes also complained of the scarcity of wood, water and provisions, and represented the Indians as being very hostile and treacherous; while, in most cases, those who traveled over the southern route experienced no hindrance, difficulty or impediment whatever, having had pleasure, peace and plenty all the way. But besides the advantages of climate, surface, soil, wood and water, there are other considerations which weigh in favor of the southern route. The distance is much shorter, and the population is more friendly, civilized and thrifty. It will bring us on more intimate terms with the Mexicans, and they will be induced to purchase larger quantities of our manufactured and imported merchandise.

Every southern man should feel a lively interest in this gigantic scheme, and enlist all his energies in aid of its completion. It affords one of the finest opportunities that the South has ever enjoyed for establishing her commercial independence, for counterbalancing the increasing commercial power of the North. In connection with this subject, I may here present an extract from a letter which I had the honor to receive, not long since, from one of the most sagacious and far-sighted patriots of the South. Speaking of the great Atlantic and Pacific Railway, among other things, he says: "North Carolina should not be an indifferent spectator of this noble enterprise. The port of Beaufort, unrivaled for health, possesses a depth of water sufficient for all convenient purposes; while the placid bosom of its well-protected harbor, justly entitles it to be styled the Pacific port of the Atlantic coast. Pursue its degree of latitude westward across the continent and the Pacific ocean, and you will find that degree passing near Memphis, Little Rock, Fulton, El Paso, and San Diego to Shanghai, the last two being the nearest ports of the two continents, in so low a latitude. Railways are chartered from Beaufort westward, and are constructed, or in progress of construction, that will reach perhaps one third or half way across the continent. May we not then hope, ere long, to see them uniting the two oceans?"

Experienced navigators have said that, in consequence of the favorable course of the trade-winds, the voyage can be accomplished between San Diego and Shanghai in about eight days' less time than it can be between San Francisco and Shanghai; and this is certainly a very strong argument in favor of running the road directly to San Diego—leaving San Francisco to the right.

Since the above was written, the following abstract of the "Report of the Secretary of War on the several Pacific Railroad Explorations" has been published; and as it more than substantiates the correctness of my remarks, and imbodies a great deal of valuable information concerning the various routes, I hope the reader will peruse it with due care and attention. I here transcribe it, with brief comments, from the columns of the *Herald:*

PACIFIC RAILROAD EXPLORATIONS.

The "Report of the Secretary of War on the several Pacific Railroad Explorations" is before us. It is an interesting and instructive document, embracing a careful review of the capabilities and drawbacks of the following routes, from the actual surveys:

FIRST—The extreme northern route, (Major Stevens',) between the 47th and 49th parallels of latitude, starting from St. Paul in Minnesota territory, and striking the Pacific at Puget's Sound, or the mouth of the Columbia, in Oregon. This will require a road, allowing for ascent and descent, of 2,207 miles. Estimated cost, $130,-871,000. The impediments in this route are the mountains to be tunneled, the numerous rivers to be bridged, the scarcity of timber, the coldness of the climate, and its proximity to the British possessions.

SECOND—Route of the forty-first parallel, (Mormon route,) commencing on the navigable waters of the Missouri, or on the Platte river, and striking thence over the Plains to the South Pass, thence to the Great Salt Lake, thence across the Great Basin to the Sierra Nevada chain, thence over that chain, and down to the Sacramento river, and down the same to Benicia, just above San Francisco, on the same harbor. Estimated distance from Council Bluffs to Benicia, 2,031 miles; estimated cost, $116,095,000. Obstructions same as in the first route, including wider deserts and deeper and rougher mountain gorges.

THIRD—Route of the thirty-eighth parallel, more familiarly known as Benton's great Central route, pronounced utterly impracticable from its mountain obstructions. Estimated length from

Westport to San Francisco, 2,080 miles. The topographical engineers gave up all estimates of the cost of a road by this route, in absolute despair.

FOURTH—Route of the thirty-fifth parallel—(Senator Rusk's route)—beginning at Fort Smith, in Arkansas, thence westward to Albuquerque on the Upper Rio Grande, thence across the Rocky Mountains and the Colorado of the West and great desert basin and its mountains, and the lower end of the Sierra Nevada chain to San Pedro, at the southern extremity of California, on the Pacific. This route is about as bad as Benton's, although the engineers think that 3,137 equated miles and $169,210,265 might, perhaps, do the work.

FIFTH—Route near the thirty-second parallel, or the extreme southern route, via Texas, New Mexico, El Paso and the Gila to the Pacific. Estimated distance from Fulton in Arkansas, to San Pedro on the Pacific, 1,618 miles—equated length, allowing for ascents and descents, 2,239 miles. Estimated cost, $68,970,000.

The advantages of this route are, that it is practically a third shorter than any of the others between the Mississippi and the Pacific—that it goes by the flank of the Rocky Mountains and the Sierra Nevada chain, instead of going over or under them—that the route is over a region of elevated table lands requiring little or no grading—and that the soil is dry and free from snow from one end to the other, except occasional light falls in New Mexico.

RECAPITULATION.

ROUTES.	Distance of Routes.	Ascents and Descents.	Length of Level Routes.	Comparative Cost.
	Miles.	*Feet.*	*Miles.*	
Extreme northern...	1,864	18,100	2,207	$130,781,000
Mormon...........	2,032	29,120	2,583	116,095,000
Benton's...........	2,080	49,986	3,125	*—
Albuquerque........	1,892	48,812	2,816	169,210,265
Extreme southern...	1,618	32,784	2,239	68,970,000

* The cost by this route is so great that the road is impracticable.

SUMMIT OF HIGHEST PASS.

	Feet.
Extreme Northern route	6,044
Tunnel at elevation of,	5,219
Northern route	8,373
Benton's route,	10,032
Tunnel at elevation of,	9,540
Albuquerque route	7,472
Extreme Southern route	5,717

These are the results of careful scientific explorations, by highly accomplished engineers, of the several routes, from the extreme Northern to the extreme Southern route; and it is only necessary to consult one of the latest maps of the United States to see at a glance that the only really available route is that of the extreme South, via El Paso and the Gadsden country. The estimated cost of a railroad (single track, we suppose) by this route is, in round numbers, $69,000,000, about half the estimate of the best of the other routes, to say nothing further of the saving of a thousand miles or so in the important matter of the distance to be traversed.

We consider this report conclusive as to the best route for a Pacific Railroad—it is the extreme Southern route. A glance on any respectable map of the United States, at the several routes indicated, will satisfy the reader of this fact. The engineers of the army have only made it more clear and satisfactory from their actual surveys.

But I must return again to my theme—California! I will now lay before the reader a few extracts from letters which I have recently received from friends in the Pacific State, and it will be seen how fully they corroborate my own statement.

An editorial friend, writing to me from San Francisco, says:—"Business all over California remains in the same stagnant condition, and every sign prognosticates a time of hardship and suffering. A crisis, in my opinion, is approaching, which will drag down nine-tenths of the business houses in the country. Money gets more stringent every day, and every body seems to be at a loss to know what to do. I must confess I see nothing promising in the future. It is truly a dark day for California."

Another correspondent says — "There have been an unusual number of murders, suicides, duels and squatter riots within the last fortnight. Heaven only knows what is to become of our people. The devil seems to have them all by the nose, and there is no telling where his double-tailed majesty means to lead them." In another letter, this same correspondent goes on to say—"I have no encouraging news to send you by this mail. Our markets continue distressingly dull. A great many failures have taken place, and others are anticipated. Indeed, these are trying times with the mercantile portion of our community. Every things wears a dull and unpromising aspect. Hundreds of mechanics and laborers, many of whom are in a deplorably destitute condition, are sauntering about the streets, having nothing to do, and being unable to find employment. And as a consequence of this unprosperous state of things, we have to contend with many cases of despair and desperation. Within the last week, four suicides, three murders, numerous robberies and other crimes have been committed in our city; and the accounts from the up-country towns, and from the interior of the State, convince us that there is less respect paid to the moral and civil laws in those places, than there is in this. It is known that there are now two large bands of highwaymen prowling about the country; and our cities are filled with secret organizations for rapacity and plunder."

Again, another correspondent says—"Every avenue to business is blocked up with a crowd waiting for an opportunity. Scores of men of almost every trade and profession are seeking employment amongst us; but there is no demand for their services. You have no idea of the number of young men who are getting themselves into a bad pickle by coming to this country. California is indeed a mammoth lottery, and the credulous world has been very impatient to secure tickets in it, refusing to believe the fact that there are ninety-nine blanks to every prize. Two earthquakes and several fires have occurred since I wrote to you from Sacramento. The earthquakes were very slight, and but little damage resulted from them; but the losses by fire have been immense. Enormous sums of foreign capital are continually passing between the Atlantic States and our city, in search of profitable investment."

The following interesting letter, just received, I give in full:—

WEAVERVILLE, Cal., May 7th, 1855.

My Dear Friend,—I owe you an *amende* for the "long and silent lapse" that has lately occurred in our correspondence—or rather in that part of it which emanates from me. A simple statement of the fact that I have been constantly on the move for the past four months is the best apology I have to offer in extenuation of my fault.

Let us retrospect a little. I wrote you frequently from Humboldt Bay, in answer to favors—my last letter having been written the day previous to my leaving that place. As I then intimated, the next day found me on my way to the mines; and the journey, rough as it was, during the most inclement season of the year, and reaching to a distance of one hundred and fifty miles, I performed *on foot!* You have a pretty good idea of the mountains of this country, and can realize the amount of fatigue and hardship attendant upon such a trip as mine. Scarcely twenty-four hours passed that it did not either rain, hail or snow, while we had not even a tent to shelter us. Yet, with all this, I improved daily in health and strength—weighing now ten pounds heavier than at any time previous.

What is to be the result, pecuniarily, of this trip, is yet to be answered. I have a mining claim, which, with all my industry and economy, has only yielded me a living. It may improve—I may make a "strike"—but this is mere speculation. Time alone can tell. I like mining much—hard work though it be—and am resolved to follow it as a business for the remnant of my days, or until I have a competence. There is a charm—an inexpressible something, inherent in the pursuit—which carries a man through the day's toil with unabated energy. It is a feeling akin to that which leads men to the gaming table, to wild speculations, or to hazardous undertakings; and each succeeding day finds a miner as eager as ever to continue the search after the hidden treasure. The gold has a different appearance, a greater intrinsic value in his eyes, than that which is acquired in any other way. He is the *first* to receive it from Nature's bank of deposit, and it possesses a beauty that no coin can equal.

It is away up on the head waters of Trinity river, or rather on one of its tributaries, that my cabin rears its humble proportions. With no neighbors nearer than one mile—the mountains rising high above and all around me—encompassed by a forest of pine and spruce—in the midst of wild beasts, wild cats, catamounts, grizzlies and lions—I am leading a genuine backwoods life. It is needless to say that its novelty charms me, and that I glory in the most perfect independence. Nor is this all. Flowers, beautiful, rich, rare, bedeck the mountain sides, (for this is May, the month of flowers,) and I can gather a bouquet that would shame those of civilized gardens. Nature defies art, and Nature's gems stand proudly, unrivaled and unapproached. And yet this is not all. There is a little bird who sits and warbles, almost all day long, the sweetest melody I ever heard. Up in the foliage of a huge pine, adjacent to my cabin, dwells the pretty songster; and I speak but the truth when I say that beside him a canary would hang its head. My wild-wood warbler reigns the king of songsters.

My furniture arrangements are not, as yet, finished. I have neither table nor chairs. Supported at one end by a sack of potatoes, at the other by my left hand, is the board on which this sheet is laid, while your humble friend sits on the ground, *a la Turk*, (or tailor,) and indites this "missel" to you. I am meek and lowly in my pretensions now, Hinton, and my rough miner's suit sits lightly on my frame. Adieu for the present. I have no envelopes, and must, therefore, close on this page. Wishing you every success and happiness,

I remain your attached friend,

* * *

And now listen to what the District Attorney for the county of San Francisco says. In a speech which he delivered some time ago in a criminal case in the city of San Francisco, he makes use of the following language:—"Twelve hundred murders have been committed in this city within the last four years, and only one of the murderers has been convicted!" What a striking comment is this upon California justice! Twelve hundred murders in the city of San Francisco alone, within the space of four years, and only one conviction! But it is unnecessary for me to lengthen my remarks upon these subjects. If additional evidences of the corruption and rottenness of affairs in California are required, all that is necessary is to look into the papers that come from that State, and the desired knowledge will soon be obtained. Here, however, let me simply say that it is impossible to get at the real, naked facts from the California journals. Almost every newspaper in the State is under the control of interested parties, and they will not allow the truth to be spoken when it conflicts with their schemes and projects. Nevertheless, enough may be learned from them to convince any reasonable person of the correctness of my description of California.

Thus, then, I have given a fair and truthful statement of what I saw, and those who are not yet convinced must go and test the matter for themselves. They will find what I have told them to be true, and that there is more enormity there than I have ventured to detail.

The absence of all social feeling, of refinement, of the little elegancies of life, is painfully manifest. It would, of course, be absurd to expect in a new country all the luxuries of an old civilization, but their absence constitutes no excuse for the total want of even the decencies of life. Law is a nullity, or at best a mere nominal thing; order does not exist except where the dread of the bowie-knife or the revolver enforces it. Men of notoriously bad character are intrusted with the management of affairs, and are easily accessible to bribery. Justice is proverbially venal, legislation is utterly corrupt. Such a loose administration of public affairs would be productive of bad results any where, but its influence is especially malign in California, where so many desperate men are to be found, determined, at every hazard, to better their fortunes. Murder, robbery and swindling are the methods by which they aim to increase their income, the law being powerless to check them.

We have called attention to the general barrenness of the soil, and endeavored to impress upon the reader's mind a conviction of the great uncertainties of mining. What then remains to attract the emigrant? The feverish excitement of speculation, which entices so many only to destroy them. In all countries, this is productive of as much loss as gain, but in California, where projects are pursued with a recklessness elsewhere unknown, the losses are on a gigantic scale. Disappointments, therefore, have the keenness of those of the beaten gambler, to whom defeat is irretrievable ruin. What wonder, then, that suicides are so common in that unhappy country?

Of the condition of females in that State, it is useless for me to speak. I have already said enough on that subject, and it becomes every man who thinks of emigrating thither, to ponder well the risks to which he will subject the ladies of his family. The enormities chargeable upon California in this respect would be difficult to parallel in any age of the world. They are of so gross a nature that it is impossible even to allude to them in a book which may be seen by women.

And now, after having well considered all these things, after having become thoroughly acquainted with the facts I have been at the pains to collect and record, I would again ask my reader, Are you going to California?

THE END.

www.ingramcontent.com/pod-product-compliance
Lightning Source LLC
LaVergne TN
LVHW010211110826
845151LV00004B/1057

* 9 7 8 1 4 2 5 5 2 8 2 7 0 *